The Best-ever Guide to the Monterey Peninsula and the Carmel Area

Fourth Edition

© 1999
By Thom Akeman

Includes a reprint of the
author's previous book,
Moving to Monterey

Published by The Kaskaskia Press
P.O. Box 1067
Pacific Grove, CA 93950

1-800-634-8444
PROACTIV

Published by The Kaskaskia Press
P.O. Box 1067
Pacific Grove, CA 93950

This book is based on the original edition of **The Best-ever Guide to the Monterey Peninsula and Carmel Area**, which was published by The Kaskaskia Press in 1994, with a second edition in 1995 and a third in 1997.

It includes a reprint of the author's previous book, **Moving to Monterey, A Newcomer's Guide to the Peninsula Paradise**, published by The Kaskaskia Press in 1988, with a second printing in 1990. Much of that work first appeared in the Sunday Weekend Magazine, published by The Monterey Peninsula Herald Co., as a series of columns called "First Impressions."

Illustrated by Irene Lagorio

ISBN 0-9623209-2-7

Your Guide to Paradise

The Monterey Peninsula-Carmel area is clearly one of the most beautiful and famous places in the world.

It attracts 8 million people each year to bask in the coastal scenery, watch the animals in the wild, bicycle along the seashore, kayak in the ocean, walk through the woods, play golf on one of the 20 local courses, eat at one of the famous restaurants, picnic or just breathe the fresh, crisp air.

I visited often before I finally got lucky and moved here in 1987. Yes, it's still a fantasy.

One of the things that used to mystify me is that there wasn't a general guidebook of the area.

Oh, there were lots of guides to particular things, like hiking trails and history. And there were some regional guides that mentioned a little about the Monterey Peninsula, like parks locations, bed-and-breakfast inns and that sort of thing.

Each community here seemed to have its own tourist brochures, most of them pointing out the shopping areas, hotels, restaurants and other places to spend money in that particular community.

And there were lots of the slick restaurant guides in the area, free magazines, papers and brochures that boast of never having a bad meal or an outrageous check. That is nothing but paid advertising, of course, even though some of it is disguised pretty well.

When I first started visiting here I found that John Steinbeck's old novels were the closest things to local guidebooks I could find. I read about Cannery Row, Tortilla Flat, Holman's Department Store and the Carmel River, places I've become quite familiar with over the years. While I would never complain about a Steinbeck novel, they really weren't any help in deciding where to have dinner on Saturday night. So I eventually decided to do a guidebook of my own. **The Best-ever Guide to the Monterey Peninsula and Carmel Area** is the result.

The First Edition was published in 1994 as the only general guidebook in the area. Now there are eight or nine on the market.

But as I finish revising this **Fourth Edition**, I really believe this is still the best-ever local guidebook in the area. A couple of the others are very good, but a couple of them are very bad. Some were actually written on the East Coast by people whose recommendations indicate they aren't familiar with this place at all. Others are local but vague. Some are wordy and unfocused. Some are simply outdated.

The Best-ever Guide to the Monterey Peninsula and Carmel Area is the most honest, I think, probably a result of my 30 years as a newspaper reporter. This one has more restaurant reviews than any of the others, has more highlights, more insights and more laughs.

It's also current, since I keep updating with new editions.

The front of the guidebook is stuff I've learned while living here — the best places to go, the best things to do.

There are also concise sections on the communities within this world-famous resort: Monterey, Carmel, Pebble Beach, Pacific Grove and Big Sur.

There are the restaurants — more than 120 of them reviewed in one fashion or another — and a section of honest wine notes, a rundown on the bars and nightlife here.

The back of the guidebook is a reprint of an earlier book titled **Moving to Monterey**. It was a collection of columns I wrote for the Monterey County Herald when I first moved here. They have proven to be timeless in this paradise.

I hope you find some good guidance, useful advice and at least some chuckles in this book. I also hope you have such a good time here you'll want to write a book of your own, or maybe an inspirational poem, or a happy song.

— *Thom Akeman*

4

INDEX to

The Best-ever Guide to the Monterey Peninsula and the Carmel Area

Introductions 3, 9, 80

Maps. 6, 7, 48, 54, 58, 60, 61

30 Great Meals for Under $10 11

29 Others Worth Knowing About 23

10 Restaurants for the View 35

The 10 or 11 Very Best Restaurants .39

10 ready-made picnics 46

SPECIAL. TOURS

    Monterey: Where History Began 49

    Pacific Grove: The Sanctuary City .52

    Pebble Beach: The Famous Drive .55

    Carmel: Bring Your Own Parking .56

    Big Sur: Far Out 59

Events and Special Attractions 62

The Best Places for Walks 66

Rent-by-the-hour Adventures 68

Best Places to Take Pictures 70

Wines Worth Drinking 73

About Bars and Nightlife Here 76

Shopping 78

"Moving to Monterey," a Special Reprint of the Book 79

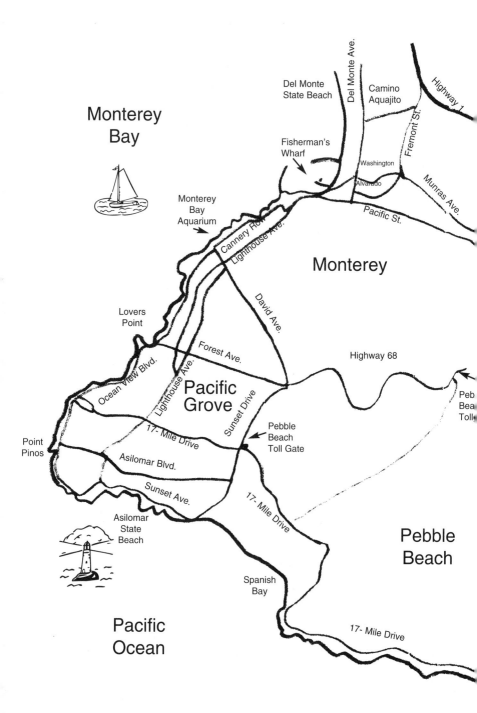

Monterey Bay

Monterey Bay Aquarium

Del Monte State Beach

Del Monte Ave.

Camino Aquajito

Highway 1

Fisherman's Wharf

Fremont St.

Washington

Alvarado

Munras Ave.

Pacific St.

Cannery Row

Lighthouse Ave.

Monterey

Lovers Point

David Ave.

Forest Ave.

Highway 68

Ocean View Blvd.

Lighthouse Ave.

Pacific Grove

Sunset Drive

Peb
Bea
Toll

Point Pinos

17- Mile Drive

Pebble Beach Toll Gate

Asilomar Blvd.

Sunset Ave.

17- Mile Drive

Asilomar State Beach

Pebble Beach

Spanish Bay

17- Mile Drive

Pacific Ocean

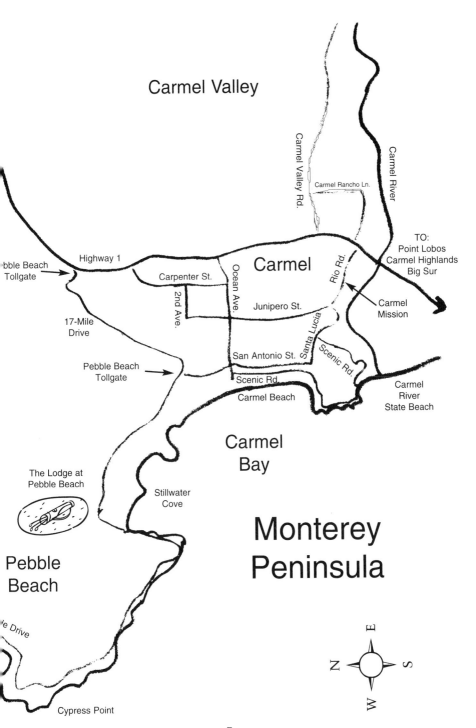

Carmel Valley

Carmel Valley Rd.

Carmel River

Carmel Rancho Ln.

TO:
Point Lobos
Carmel Highlands
Big Sur

Highway 1

bble Beach
Tollgate

Carpenter St.

Ocean Ave.

Carmel

Rio Rd.

2nd Ave.

Junipero St.

Carmel
Mission

17-Mile
Drive

Santa Lucia

San Antonio St.

Scenic Rd.

Pebble Beach
Tollgate

Scenic Rd.

Carmel Beach

Carmel
River
State Beach

Carmel
Bay

The Lodge at
Pebble Beach

Stillwater
Cove

Monterey
Peninsula

Pebble
Beach

e Drive

Cypress Point

N   E   S   W

7

EATING ON A BUDGET

Food Guide
For Paradise

There are about 300 places to eat in the Monterey Peninsula-Carmel area and half of them are pretty good.

Some are real bargains.

Others charge the price of a diamond ring for a meal you'd rather not eat.

Every resort that has lots of tourists passing through has its share of overpriced traps that don't cater to repeat business. This one is no exception. There are restaurants here with expensive crap coming out of their kitchens.

There are also places that charge a lot and are worth every penny, and places that almost give good food away.

This book is intended to help you figure out which is which.

You don't have to risk a bad meal while you're here, or search for the Burger King or live on cheese and crackers. I've got lists that will steer you to good food at right prices.

I've eaten in almost all of the restaurants in Monterey, Pacific Grove, Pebble Beach, Carmel, Carmel Valley and Big Sur so I've pretty well sorted the good from the bad, the reasonable prices from the gouges and the absolute exquisite from the pretentious.

I've also paid for my own meals, so my opinions are as honest as the veteran newspaper reporter in me can make them. They won't sound like the paid advertising you're bombarded with here.

There are some 50 places here that will charge you $100 for a dinner for two. I've had some meals that are worth that, others that I'm still mad about. There are also places here where you can have memorable meals for $5.

A true find would be a place with great food, cheap prices and stunning views all under one roof. I haven't found any of those during my years in the area, but I have found some okay places with stunning views, some viewless places that serve great food and some terrific restaurants that are wonderfully cheap.

It may be arguable whether I'm a gourmet, but I do like to eat, I know what tastes good and I know the difference between truly fresh seafood and something caught in a microwave oven. I hate price gouging, shoddy or arrogant service and restaurants with less ambience than Greyhound bus stations.

To help you sort out my standards I'll tell you that I agree with only about a third of the high ratings provided by the popular Mobil Travel Guide, which has awarded 25 of the restaurants here with at least three stars. I believe that about a third of the Mobil three-stars are really better than that, while the other third shouldn't be allowed to feed people.

Several of the highly-rated restaurants here have pretty ordinary food. Two of the Mobil three-stars are actually tasteless unless you add a lot of salt and pepper. One makes everything swim in olive oil. One serves fish after it's gone cold and ice cream after it's gone warm. One serves garbage in a devine setting. And one is owned by a creep.

The Best-ever Guide to the Monterey Peninsula and Carmel Area is much more reliable than Mobil. Or any other guide, for that matter.

There are honest differences, of course. I have friends that I generally trust who swear by a place in Pacific Grove named **Fandango**. It is popular and routinely gets good reviews from people like the Mobil critics. But I've been there four times and I've had four bad experiences. At those prices I have trouble thinking of a fifth visit.

I might note that I offered my first list of favorite restaurants in 1987, when I listed 10 in a weekly column I wrote for The Herald. Of those, four are still among my favorites — Rio Grill, Rosine's, First Awakenings (old name: First Watch) and Peppers, all of which have maintained their quality over the years. Two of my other early favorites have gone out of business and the rest have been replaced by better choices I've found.

As a footnote, let me say that restaurant prices seem to have doubled over the years, while the food has gotten more and more varied. Local wine prices have nearly tripled, but the products have gotten a world better. My guess is that real estate prices, values, financing and rates have been the biggest factor in driving up food prices, that and the increased demand for good wine.

With that, here are my lists of favorite restaurants, places where you can get:
- 30 great meals for less than $10;
- 29 really good meals for a little more;
- 10 okay meals in stunning settings;
- 10 or 11 memorable dinners at the very best of the pricey restaurants here; and
- 10 ready-made picnics at handy take-out places.

30 Great Meals for under $10

There is some wonderful food in the Monterey Peninsula-Carmel area for little more than pocket change, if you just know where to find it.

There are great breakfasts, relaxing lunches and memorable dinners that will keep anybody's budget intact.

Here's where you can find them:

DOWNTOWN MONTEREY

Rosine's Restaurant is in the heart of downtown Monterey. It's at 434 Alvarado St., which is about two blocks from the Doubletree and Marriott hotels. There are movie theaters, book stores, shops, clubs and coffeehouses in that area.

This is a big place that I can best describe as an old-fashioned restaurant, with spacious booths along the walls, tables on the main floor and small, tables for two at front windows that open onto the street.

You need to be warned that the dessert case is right inside the front door, so you have to walk by large, ornate cakes, tall meringue and mounds of luscious-looking brownies as you go in. It always makes my teeth ache.

The restaurant is open from morning to night. Lunch hours are always crowded because this is one of the favorite places for the people who work in downtown Monterey.

The food is reliably good, the service quick and the prices right.

The menu is diverse. My favorites are the turkey sandwiches made from fresh-roasted turkeys. There's a "Satch's original turkey dip" that is turkey breast on a sweet roll, with au jus to dip it into. It's about $7.

I also like the salads — a garden patch, which is a huge plate of vegetables smothered with sprouts, kidney beans, garbonzas and avocado.

And Rosine's makes my favorite minestrone soup.

The pastas are about $9 each, the salads and sandwiches about $8.

Jugem at 409 Alvarado St. is a decent Japanese restaurant that always provides a quiet, calm respite.

It has a sushi bar that offers varieties of raw fish that I will never knowingly eat. Those seem to start at $3 a serving, so your bill follows your appetite.

11

But the box dinners, as they are called, are a good deal at $6.75. They include soup, slaw, rice and two entrees. My favorites are tempura vegetables and chicken teriyaki. Of course the menu offers a full range of tempuras, meats, noodles and soups, most for under $10. The most expensive dishes in the house are sushi platters, which range up to $17.

Papa Chano's at 462 Alvarado St. is a fast-food, Mexican restaurant that many of my friends swear by.

I don't think it's that good. In fact, I think that if they left the pepper out of Papa Chano's food it would be tasteless, which isn't what Mexican usually is.

But I've given up trying to fight the crowd. I go to this place because the prices are low ($7 for an enchilada dinner with the works), the portions are huge (a $5.45 super burrito you can't possibly eat at one sitting), the place is open late (until 11 p.m.) and the whole thing is fast (in case you're trying to catch a movie down the street, or beat the meter maid to your car).

Tutto Buono at 469 Alvarado St. is a simple, straightforward Italian restaurant that can stuff you with pasta for as little as $7.

The menu uses lots of fancy words for olive oil and rosemary, but the food is the kind you'd make at home if you had the time and inclination.

It has a full range of pastas, pizza, salads and sandwiches in the $7 to $9 range for lunch, the $10 to $12 range for dinner.

Tutto Buono is popular with downtown workers, probably the second choice to only Rosine's. It can be busy, especially at lunch time, but it's a huge place with extra tables tucked behind wine racks and lined up beside the bar in back.

Epsilon restaurant at 422 Tyler St. is a block or two off the beaten path, but it's well worth the effort to find it. It's a Greek cafe just a block down from Alvarado, a few doors east of Franklin.

Epsilon is a charming and sparkling clean cafe with large windows across the front, mirrors, paintings and murals on the walls, curtains and plants hanging from the ceiling.

The food is great and the servings are large. Full meals are $6 to $8 at lunchtime, $10 to $15 at dinnertime. They include beans, peas, lentils, carrots, rice, salad and, of course, pita bread.

You could predict the lamb, eggplant, grape leaves and feta cheese dishes, but I don't think you could predict how good they are. My favorite, so far, is the gyros, spiced beef and lamb in pita bread for about

$6, on a platter for about $10. I would also recommend the houmos as a unique appetizer, $3.95.

Turtle Bay Taqueria at 451 Tyler St. is sort of across from Epsilon, at the corner of Tyler and Bonifacio Place in downtown Monterey. It's a spinoff of the highly-successful Fishwife restaurants in Pacific Grove and Seaside.

Turtle Bay, like its sister in Seaside, is a brightly-colored, order-at-the-counter place that serves Yucatan-inspired food — seafood over a bowl of rice, wrapped in a burrito or plopped into a taco.

It's different for a fast-food place, but it's reliably good, nutritious and relatively inexpensive. Bowls and wraps are in the $5 range.

India's Clay Oven at 150 Del Monte Ave., just down the street from the Doubletree Hotel and the Marriott of Monterey, has one of the best lunch buffets in the area.

It is Indian food, obviously, spicy, tasty and sometimes hot. The real advantage of the buffet, I think, is that you get to pick your own level of heat from a wide variety of dishes that range from fiery mushrooms to sweet rice pudding. But the $7.45 buffet is only available for weekday lunches.

There is a full menu of Indian food for dinners and on weekends. The waiters are helpful in describing the dishes to people not familiar with Indian cuisine, which is dominated by vegetables, yogurts, cottage cheeses, chicken, lamb, rices and breads.

My very favorite is a mouth-watering chicken korma, a creamy curry priced at $9.75 ala carte, $11.75 for the full dinner.

India's Clay Oven is on the second floor of a building that is part of the city's massive parking complex. Over the rooftops and parked cars, there is a fetching view of Monterey Bay and the boats in the marina.

Siamese Bay Restaurant at 131 Webster St., behind the Monterey Post Office, is one of the good Thai restaurants in the area. (Note: There are a couple of good ones and a couple of lousy ones. I'd follow this guide, if I were you.)

If you want a bargain lunch, hit their $5.95 smorgasbord. It's got a nice selection of vegetables, meat and noodle dishes, even if they are a little hot for me.

On their regular menu, I sort of head for the chicken curries in the $6.95 range. Seafood and duck specialties can run up to $15.

I personally avoid the spiciest dishes in Thai restaurants because the

13

one time I went for broke, I got all the symptoms of a heart attack.
I've stuck to the milder side of the spices since then. Sometimes I even
have Pahd Thai, which is a dish of sweet noodles, peanuts and sprouts.

Duffy's Tavern is right next to a side gate of the Army Presidio at 282
High St. It serves the best hamburgers I've found in the area, in a conge-
nial little setting that always helps relax me.

The place gets around $7 for its burgers, which are huge and have spe-
cial names like The Churchill (covered with melted cheddar) and The
Tearjerker (loaded with grilled onions).

The burgers come with lots of French fries or a crisp salad.

It is a pub, so there are lots of beers to pick from. I wouldn't recommend the house wine, nor the coffee. But for a burger and a beer, this is
the place.

AQUARIUM AREA/CANNERY ROW

First Awakening is in the American Tin Cannery in Pacific Grove,
near the Monterey Bay Aquarium and the Monterey-Pacific Grove line,
at 125 Ocean View Blvd.

This little place has an outdoor courtyard with big tables, umbrellas
and lots of real birds flying in and out. It also has indoor rooms with
booths and tables, but they tend to be noisy.

It's only open for breakfast and lunch and usually has a waiting line at
prime times.

The pancakes are divine. When the berries are available, First Awakenings
has blueberry pancakes that have more fruit in them than batter.

The omelettes are imaginative, the fruit bowls pretty and the rest of
the menu quite acceptable.

My personal favorite is an open-face sandwich called chicken little. It's
lumpy chicken breast mixed in mayonnaise and raisins, spread on an
English muffin and covered by melted cheese. First Awakenings serves it
with wonderfully fried potatoes and a small salad.

The chicken little is $5.75, the pancakes about $5, omelettes about $6.

If you try the place, you'll go back again.

Sea Harvest Fish Market & Restaurant at 598 Foam St. across
Hoffman Avenue from the Cannery Row Parking Garage, is one of the
least-discovered great cafes in Monterey, even if it's only five blocks from
the aquarium.

I had been in and out of it for years because that's where I buy most of
my fish. The store generally has the biggest selection of fresh fish in the

14

area, and a good catch of whatever came out of Monterey Bay that day.

I had noticed the dozen tables at the side of the store, but I never saw many people there so I never thought much about it as a restaurant. Until I ate there one day. Wow, what great seafood!

The cafe itself is simple and plain, with windows that look out on passing traffic. But the food is terrific.

You want the fish, of course, as an entree, a sandwich, an appetizer, a soup or spread on a salad. My favorite is fried squid on a French roll with a side of the cole slaw that contains raisins and pine nuts. That's $8.95. Full fish dinners (with anything in the seafod case) are in the $12 range.

The place isn't open late, only until 8 p.m. on weeknights, 9 p.m. on weekends. And I should warn you the coffee can be iffy.

There's a sister Sea Harvest in The Crossroads shopping center at Highway 1 and Rio Road – same fish market focus, even simpler cafe. And there's another in Salinas.

Lighthouse Bistro at 401 Lighthouse Ave. in what is called New Monterey (the streets above Cannery Row), is one of those jewels everyone is afraid will be overrun. It is the simple, charming venture of people who like food well enough to serve excellent dishes in large portions at low prices.

They did this in a larger restaurant in an industrial park on the outskirts of town a few years ago, a place that quickly grew into one of the area's busiest and most popular eateries without a penny spent on advertising. From there they fell back into a sandwich shop in New Monterey and, more recently, opened this gem of a little restaurant.

Lunch is ordered at the deli counter right inside the door, then brought to your table in the dining room or on the patio out front.

I love the sesame chicken breast — a huge sandwich covered in fried onions and provolone. But there's always an intriguing selection of other sandwiches like fish, mushroom, turkey, pork or duck, and a variety of salads and burritos in the $7 to $8 range.

Basque dinners are served family style, with bowls of vegetables and such to accompany individually selected entrees. They go from $12 to $16.

Gianni's Pizza at 725 Lighthouse Ave., a few blocks up from the aquarium, has become an institution. There's an almost-continual jam in the parking lot when the place is open – evenings and weekends.

The pizza's not that good, really, but the restaurant has a wholesome aura of Little League about it that says my dad's team ate here when they won and, by God, so will mine.

I find the pizza greasy, but it's loaded with generous portions of meats and things. And I seem to be the only one in town with any reservations about it.

Grand China is an unpretentious Chinese restaurant at 738 Lighthouse Ave. in a little place called New Monterey Center across from Gianni's Pizza.

Everything on the menu is under $10, including the shrimp dishes. Most of the entrees are $6 to $8 and loaded with stir-fried vegetables. The menu is fairly standard, but the kitchen is more Mandarin than Szechuan so if you want your food firey, say so.

This little place is simple and decent. But one of the very best things about it is that it delivers all over Monterey, Pacific Grove and Pebble Beach, even to the hotels and motels.

Tillie Gort's at 111 Central Ave. in Pacific Grove is getting pretty close to veggie heaven.

Oh, it has meats and things, but the heavy emphasis here is on the interesting soups, salads and sandwiches you can make with vegetables and a little imagination. I consider it "a sprout house" and a place I like to touch base with every once in a while.

I avoid the whole-wheat tortillas because I think there's something wrong with the concept, just as I avoid the veggie burger.

But I've had some wonderful salads with honey dressings at Tillie's, plates of stir-fried vegetables and even the turkey sandwich, which utilizes pita bread.

The gentle place seems to get even better with time. And where else can you hear the Eagles on the stereo while you're waiting?

MONTEREY OUTSKIRTS

Crazy Horse Restaurant is the unlikely name of the best salad bar in the area. It is the restaurant at the Bay Park Hotel at 1425 Munras Ave. in Monterey, just off the Highway 1 freeway.

This is a restaurant with full menu and bar. But in the couple of hundred times that I've been there, I don't believe that I've ever had anything but the salad bar.

The reason is simple. This place sets out a better variety of fresh vegetables than any other so-called salad bar in the area. There's a good selection of raw vegetables with salad dressings, cheeses, fresh turkey and lean ham, nuts and toppings to go with them. You can have a salad here that's as good as you want to make it.

The salad bar also has several deli salads on it like macaroni salad and potato salad, always some fresh fruit and soup.

It comes with a wonderful bread that is loaded with poppy, sunflower and sesame seeds.

It's a favorite meal for about $8.

Chef Lee's Mandarin House is just north of Highway 1 on Monterey's North Fremont Street.

It may not be the best Chinese food you've ever had, but it's as good as Mandarin gets this side of San Francisco.

When I get a real hankering for Chinese food, Chef Lee's is usually where I end up. It's got the full menu, from $1 egg rolls and $5 soups to chicken, pork and beef dishes that range from $8 to $11.

I'm partial to the kung pao chicken and oyster sauce beef, both for about $8. And there's a $4.95 lunch special that can't be beat.

PACIFIC GROVE

Fishwife Seafood Restaurants offer a choice of locations. There's one in Pacific Grove, a pleasant restaurant at 1996 Sunset Drive, just across from the Asilomar Conference Center, that serves great food within view of the ocean. There's another one in Seaside, a simpler delicatessen-cafe in a commercial district at 789 Trinity Ave., which is at the corner of Fremont Boulevard, three or four blocks south of Broadway.

Both have equally wonderful food and both are usually crowded at peak meal times.

As the name implies, the Fishwifes are basically fish houses, offering a good variety that always seems fresh. They package them as entrees, sandwiches, pasta sauces and salad toppings.

The Fishwife-made pasta is melt-in-your-mouth quality. The sandwiches come with "air fries," which are delightfully greaseless French fries.

I like most of the Fishwife menu, but I have two absolute favorites. There is what they call a "sea garden salad," which is a plate of lettuce, slaw, greens and broccoli with a vinegary dressing and a slice of fish on top. I like it with a piece of red snapper, fried in the peppery Cajun style. I also love the black beans at the Fishwife and suggest they are worth ordering as a side dish if they aren't otherwise on your plate.

Daily specials — with tilapia, sole, calamari etc. — start under $10. The sea garden salad is about $8, fettuccine with lots of stuff is about $10.

Peppers Mexicali Cafe at 170 Forest Ave., in the old home-town atmosphere of Pacific Grove, is one of the best buys for the money.

The menu is sort of Mexican, in that it has taco and burrito dishes. But it's heavy on seafood and offers a number of meals prepared with the fresh catches of the day.

Not all the meals are under $10, but enough are to qualify Peppers for this listing.

For example, a taco-type thing with a full dinner (black or refried beans, rice, tortillas, chips and salsa) costs $6.50, while two main things (like a taco and burrito) is $8.95 and three cost $10.95.

The seafood specials at Peppers usually start at $8.95 and sometimes go to about twice that.

Whenever there's fresh salmon, I have them fix it up in a taco. Damn, that's good.

I've had a lot of meals at Peppers, as have most of my friends, and I've never found food there disappointing.

When it's crowded, which is usually the case at mealtime, it can be noisy and not the greatest place in the world to try to have a conversation.

Then, too, it's not a great place for dieters, because the tortilla chips Peppers puts out on the tables are irresistible. I always dip them in the green salsa because the red is fire in the throat.

Toasties Cafe in downtown Pacific Grove sits at 702 Lighthouse Ave., just across the street from the picturesque post office and cattycornered from the Shell gas station.

It is one of the favorite breakfast places on the Monterey Peninsula and usually has a waiting line out front.

It's obvious why Toasties is a favorite. It serves terrific food at reasonable prices in a clean, pleasant place. It's a model for the industry.

The restaurant is open for lunch and I wander in occasionally for a patty melt. It's also open for dinner, which I frankly haven't tried.

But for breakfast, I'm a regular.

The eggs Benedict at $6.75 is the most popular single order at Toasties, but I think the $5.75 huevos rancheros are better.

I don't think you can go wrong with the crisp bacon, the buttermilk pancakes or the pecan waffles either.

I admit to my share of fruit bowls, always a tasty variety of fresh fruit. And I've watched a friend eat a lot of hash at Toasties, which always differs with just whatever is available in the kitchen.

This, one of my alltime favorites, is well worth a wait in line.

Red House Café at 662 Lighthouse Ave., just a block up from Toasties, ✔ helps makes Pacific Grove one of the best breakfast and lunch spots on the Monterey Peninsula.

This funky old house — which was saved from demolition a few years ago by the two women who opened Miss Trawick's Garden Shop in the basement — has been reborn with superb food that almost defies characterization.

For breakfast it's hard to beat the Belgian waffles, though they are small for my appetite. For lunch, there's always homemade soup, serious salads and luscious sandwiches on breads that include foccacia. Prices are in the $6 range.

If it's a nice day, sit on a porch of the 19th century cottage and watch the birds flutter in the nearby trees.

The one drawback to the Red House is the way food is ordered. You have to stop right inside the front door to order while others are trying to get out and waiters are going back and forth with plates and pitchers. Fortunately most people are friendly, so neither fights nor romances occur as everybody crowds through that same doorway.

Petra Restaurant at 477 Lighthouse Ave. in Pacific Grove proves that there's no such thing as too many Greek restaurants.

There's a refreshing lunch or dinner here, except on Sundays, of excellent lamb — or chicken, beef or garbanzo beans, if you're in that mood — with some pita bread, fresh veggies and feta cheese. The gyros is my favorite, but there's always shish kabob and the trimmings — grape leaves, houmos and couscous.

It's good food at good prices in a clean little café. I'd try to sit near the windows in order to watch the world pass by. Lunches are in the $7 to $10 range, dinners $10 to $14.

Fifi's Cafe and French Bakery is at 1188 Forest Ave., in a little shopping center loaded with restaurants, right beside the Safeway store at the top of Forest Hill.

It's a good place to grab takeout, cookies, custards and tarts, or to have a good, substantial meal in an unpretentious cafe with cozy curtains on all the windows.

Fifi's has inventive things on the menu like lamb sandwiches, duck with blueberry sauce and chicken with raisins.

This is one of the few places in the area where you can get a good breakfast ($7 to $9), lunch ($9 to $14) or dinner ($9 to $17).

19

I'm partial to the sesame chicken salad — $8.95 for 318 calories worth of good taste you can stuff yourself on.

Allegro Gourmet Pizzeria sits at the back of the little shopping center on Forest Hill, technically at 1184 Forest Ave. If you're in the mood for a pizza, it's really worth seeking out.

On the Carmel side of the hill, the owners have a second restaurant in The Barnyard shopping center, which sits alongside Highway 1 between Carmel Valley and Rio Roads.

But I like the Pacific Grove version, mostly because I like to sneak up to the back of the upper dining room, where I've never seen anyone but my party and the help.

The Allegro pizza is some of the best around, but I say that as someone who believes there's no really good pizza west of Chicago.

Allegro has all that modern stuff, like whole-wheat crust and lots of vegetable toppings. It also has sausages and pepperonis for we old-fashioned meat eaters. Overall, there's a freshness to the pizza that sets it apart.

I like to eat it there, so I can grab a bottle of chianti and sit in the upper dining room to wait for it to cook.

The pizzas start at about $9 for a small with just cheese, and go to more than $20 for a large seafood, which I've never had. My favorite is the vegetarian, capped with artichoke hearts.

The Allegros have other foods to eat there or take out, but I've always gone for the pizza.

CARMEL

Katy's Place on Mission Street in Carmel is almost a tradition. It sits between 5th and 6th avenues, just up from the firehouse, Devendorf Park and the branch library. It serves breakfast and lunch and closes early in the afternoon. It's frequently crowded and sometimes has a waiting line.

There are some tables out front under the tall pines, which can't be beaten on a warm day. But the interior of the restaurant is pleasant enough anyway.

I've never heard of a bad meal here or an empty coffee cup.

I usually have one of the egg dishes, but I'm partial to their pancakes with fruit in them, which usually cost about $8.

The **Little Swiss Cafe** sits at the rear of the city library on 6th Avenue, between Dolores and Lincoln streets.

It is a pleasant, out-of-the-way place that makes the kinds of breakfasts and lunches that bring people back for more. It offers good food at right prices. Unfortunately, the cafe is closed in the evening, as are a lot of good eateries in Carmel. That makes good dinners at reasonable prices hard to find in this resort.

Little Swiss Cafe has a couple of small rooms to it, one with tables next to the windows of 6th Avenue, one in the back with booths.

The house specialty is cheese blintzes for $5. But I like the hash. With a couple of eggs and yummy pancakes, it's $6.50.

The Carmel Bakery on Ocean Avenue, between Dolores and Lincoln streets, has some of the best pastries I've been able to find in this area.

The bakery also has a selection of delicatessen sandwiches — on great bread, naturally — for about $6.

You can take the bakery's goodies to your car, room or on a picnic, of course. Or you can eat them there.

I should also point out that the luscious pastries and rolls that fill the bakery's front window are big and loaded with raisins, nuts and things. They are priced at about $2.

The Cottage Restaurant is a charming little place on Lincoln near 7th, next to the Church of the Wayfarer.

It offers the cozy, unrushed feel of a country inn, a rarity in Carmel. There are two rooms, one arranged around the hearth, with deacon's benches along the walls and pink chairs around the tables.

The food is good. If you want a different eggs Benedict, have one with chicken breast and avocado for about $8.

Look for the breakfast crepes in the $8 range.

Or try the artichoke soup for $5 a bowl.

Sandwiches and salads are in the $7-$8 range.

Dinners are served on Thursday, Friday and Saturday nights, with about half the items on the menu under $10.

From Scratch is on the bottom level of The Barnyard shopping center alongside Highway 1, between Rio and Carmel Valley Roads.

It has a patio area and indoor tables in a pleasant location and that's mainly why I go there. It's cozy and relaxing.

I always think of it as a breakfast place, even though it's open in the afternoon and, in summers, for dinner.

There are plenty of pancake dishes, but there are also salads, sandwiches and pastas. I definately recommend the Corralitas ham as the best in the U.S. The prices are generally in the $7 range.

BIG SUR

River Inn Resort on Highway 1, about a 30-minute drive south of Carmel, is at the heart of Big Sur.

The restaurant is surrounded by stores, a gas station and motels, so there are always people around and others coming and going.

The restaurant has a bar, features live music at times and has a large patio alongside the Big Sur River, which runs through the woods out back.

It's a very relaxing place, with all the naturalness and casualness of Big Sur.

And it serves a good plate of bacon and eggs for $7. A burger with fries is $8.50, while other sandwiches are in the $10 range. Dinners run close to $15.

29 Others Worth Knowing About

There are a lot of other restaurants in the Monterey Peninsula-Carmel area worth knowing about. Some of them serve wonderful food at fair prices, just not under my arbitrary $10 line. And some of them are near-great, some nearly the best.

Here's a list of 29 of them:

DOWNTOWN MONTEREY

Montrio restaurant in an old firehouse at 414 Calle Principal got off to an unfair start. Esquire Magazine named it the "best new restaurant" in America in 1995, an instant reputation that is difficult to live up to.

I grant you the place can be very good, but I don't think it's consistent. One whole side of the place is so noisy it's difficult to carry on a conversation. And the food is sometimes not as good as it is at others. I don't think discomfort or mediocrity is acceptable at these prices.

Don't get me wrong, Montrio is worth trying. The people who opened and own it have never been involved in a bad restaurant.

But I would ask for a booth on the quieter side, and I would ask the waiter for honest advice on what is good today.

FISHERMAN'S WHARF AREA

Cafe Fina, is one of the few restaurants I recommend on Fisherman's Wharf. It is one of the classics in Monterey.

It looks cumbersome from the front, junked up with carry-out counters, fish, pizza displays and the like. But a narrow corridor leads through that clutter to a very comfortable dining room dominated by windows looking out over water, boats and beach.

The seafood, which is in the $15 range, is some of the best in Monterey. Try seafood crepes. Or anything with their creamy tomato sause on it.

Abalonetti Seafood Trattoria right next door has been overhauled to eliminate the clutter around the front.

It looks more like a restaurant and is a good one. Tables rim the picture windows, while displays of food sit on the counter in front of the cooks, soon-to-eats sip wine at the small bar in the corner.

The restaurant, once popularized as a Clint Eastwood hangout, is now owned by John Pisto, deservedly one of the most celebrated cooks in the area. There is a wide menu, with lunch prices in the $10 to $15 range, dinner in the $15 to $20 range calamari – or squid – has been the house specialty for nearly 50 years – French fried, grilled, sauteed, breaded, stuffed, filets, strips or rings. I like it fried with the "starch of the day" pasta.

AQUARIUM AREA/CANNERY ROW

Toyota Shushi Bar at 867 Wave St. is one of the best bargains in the area. You can stuff yourself with sushi for only $6.95 at lunchtime, $13.50 at dinnertime.

It's the only place I know of where you get a controlled price for all the raw-fish delicacies you've ever wanted. I don't understand how they can do it, but I'm glad that they can.

The place is very simple. It's a small restaurant that seats only about 20 people at a time, on benches crowded in a semicircle around a chef in the center.

The sushi is delivered in an unusual cafeteria style — on the bellies of the cutest wooden otters, which float around the semicircle in a water trough.

Whaling Station Inn Restaurant at 763 Wave St. is one of the classiest restaurants in town, serving dinner the way it was meant to be, with good drinks, good selections and good cooks.

Prides itself as a steak house these days, but offers plenty of seafoods and pastas. The steaks are in the $30 range, the other meals about $20.

It's John Pisto's place, one of four owned by the guy who has tried to make himself the Monterey chef, the king of seafood, pasta, mushrooms and, now, steaks. He's close enough for my money.

The steaks here come with potatoes mashed with garlic or fried with onions and peppers.

The restaurant itself is very comfortable and unpretentious, with a huge bar at one end, colorful posters and paintings on the walls and tables along the windows that overlook Cannery Row buildings.

MONTEREY OUTSKIRTS

El Palomar at 724 Abrego St. sits near the downtown end of Munras Avenue, a motel row that runs between downtown Monterey and the Highway 1 ramps.

Avenue, a motel row that runs between downtown Monterey and the Highway 1 ramps.

It's a Mexican restaurant worth knowing about, even if it's in a huge building and has uncomfortable chairs.

El Palomar is a real Mexican restaurant that serves only refried beans, no black.

It is the only place I've ever encountered that offers squid (calamari) ceviche. There's octopus ceviche, too, for about $10.

While the fare seems dominated by seafood — heavy on prawns in all styles — it also has a considerable selection of vegetarian dishes.

I like the tacos with red snapper, which are rolled in cone shapes for $12 a meal.

Tarpy's Roadhouse is one of the "hot spots" in Monterey, attracting the sports car set and people who drink water with names.

It's a little remote, sitting off the Monterey-Salinas Highway (Highway 68) intersection with Canyon Del Rey Boulevard, about a mile east of the Monterey Peninsula Airport. And it requires a difficult left turn on a busy, two-lane highway.

But the food is worth the trouble of getting there. Tarpy's is a sister of the Rio Grill and Montrio and, like them, has some inventive stuff on the menu. There's a barbecue sauce made from apricots, for example, which is spread under a chicken breast cooked in chili butter, served with scalloped potatoes that use Gruyere cheese, and cornbread with jalapeno peppers shaped as a cactus. That's about $10 at lunchtime, $15 at dinner, and it's terrific.

Then there's a chicken breast sandwich served on cornbread, a pasta seasoned with saffron and a relish made from beer and onions.

Tarpy's is in a stone building that sits against a hillside. There are a half-dozen small dining rooms inside, a terrific patio in pleasant weather.

I prefer the patio because Tarpy's sits on the landing path to the adjacent airport. I'm uncomfortable inside when a plane roars overhead and I can't see it. I get an impulse to crawl under the table and hide. When I'm outside and can look up and see how high the plane really is, I don't mind it nearly so much.

Billy Quon's Rotisserie at Ryan Ranch is worth the drive to the outskirts of Monterey. It's in an industrial park off the Monterey-Salinas Highway, a quarter-mile east of Tarpy's, about a mile east of the Monterey Peninsula Airport.

It's one of those contemporary California places that only a veteran restauranteur like Billy Quon Lee (original owner of the Rio Grill) could put together well.

You can get crispy duck or grilled lamb, for example, on the same menu that offers Szechwan ribs and stir-fried seafood, a meal in a wok, pizza and a dynamite Cobb's salad.

The duct work is exposed and there are lots of windows, like you might expect in an industrial park, but the place is softened by the pastels, the linens and more silverware than I've ever known when to use.

It's a good place that will cost about $10 for lunch, $25 for dinner.

PACIFIC GROVE

Thai Bistro II at 159 Central Ave. is the classy Thai restaurant in the area, with a complex menu of wonderful food and pleasant staff to help you chose from it.

The restaurant is in a converted house, just a few blocks from the aquarium.

I'd start with a Sa-Tay, a skewered chicken with lime and curry sauce that pops open your taste buds. If I couldn't see anything better, I'd go on with a chili and basil sauce dish to really pull in the flavors of Thailand.

You'll find entrees in the $8 to $12 range, and a good selection of local wines and imported beers.

If you happen to be in Carmel Valley at the settlement they call The Village, you can try the original Thai Bistro. It is so good it needed to be cloned.

Pasta Mia Trattoria at 481 Lighthouse Ave., near the movie theaters downtown, gets rave reviews from some people I know who know good food.

I don't quite get it. It's in a nice old house and the folks are friendly enough, but I've never found their food worth getting excited about.

I'd stick to the basics, like linguini or lasagna, usually in the $12 to $15 range. But if this is the best restaurant you find here, you need to read this guidebook closer.

Vito's Italian Restaurant is in the Forest Hill Shopping Center at 1180 Forest Ave., near Fifi's and Allegro, two of the Great Ones where you can eat for less than $10.

Vito's is a little more expensive and, if you like authentic Sicilian cooking, well worth it. We're heavy on tomato and cheese sauces here, in a relaxing little cafe that may not have a single yuppie in it. Study the mural that fills an entire wall, depicting Vito's seaside village in Sicily.

I'm partial to the $13 ravioli, will have the $12 lasagna again and can recommend the $12 fettuccine or gnocchi without hesitation. Of course, I always have a bottle of merlot with it, which runs the price up noticeably.

Asilomar Conference Center on the coastline at 800 Asilomar Ave. offers a different kind of dining experience — camp style, lunch in a dining hall under the pines.

Asilomar is a state-owned park facility that is used principally for educational conferences. It rents out its 300 oceanside rooms at what amounts to discount rates on the Monterey Peninsula (roughly $100 a day) and throws in the rustic dining hall for three meals a day.

You don't have to be participating in a conference to eat there, or to rent a room, for that matter. A walk-in pays about $8 for lunch, $13 for dinner, to sit at a table for 10 and eat a meal that's better than those you remember from youth camp. Lunches might feature salads or stews with pizza or ham sandwiches, milk and desert. Dinners can be good — a chicken cordon bleu that I would boast about, grilled salmon that you could pay twice as much for in town.

While you're eating in the redwood lodge full of tables, you get to look through the large windows at the pines that tower above, the sand dunes that nestle around you and, from some tables, the Pacific Ocean that's just across the street.

CARMEL

Grasing's across from the fire station at 6th Avenue and Mission Street is an excellent addition to the Carmel restaurant array. I think it's one of the best of the bunch.

The place is done café-style with most of the walls given to windows on the street and a courtyard, simple tables and chairs, an outdoor patio and restrooms across the courtyard, in another building.

The food is just as straight-forward, but mixed and matched so creatively it's hard to believe such every day foods can provide such wonderful tastes. For instance, I never would have thought to cook a tuna steak with bok choy, tomatoes and garlic. It's really good that way. All the sauces — and soups — I've had at this place are just as remarkable. They enliven routine meats in delightful ways.

Dinners are in the $20 range, appetizers and deserts around $5. There is a three-course, fixed-price dinner for $25, an option becoming more common in restaurants here. I'd recommend ordering off the menu, though, to be sure you can get their calamari and onion appetizers.

Yummy, yummy!

And just to underscore why I love this place, it's menu uses one page for food, two to list the wines. It's owned by chef Kurt Grasings and Narsai David, a rightfully famous foodie in the San Francisco Bay Area.

Piatti Ristorante at 6th and Junipero avenues, right across from the downtown park, is a delightful, modern restaurant where all the cooking is out in the open.

There are a number of items on the Piatti menu that come close to my $10 line, just not under.

Their portions tend to be small, so people like me have to pay extra for salads, soups and desserts to make a meal. But in this case, that's not a complaint. The food is so good here, I've never felt overcharged.

The Piatti ravioli in lemon cream sauce my main stay. The lasagna is also notable.

PortaBella on Ocean Avenue west of Lincoln is a delightful café that says European all through it.

The dining areas — two inside and two outside — are cozy. The menu — from corn bisque to duck-filled ravioli — is intriguing. And the food is really good.

The dead singers on the sound system and the noise from an adjoining bistro are a bit distracting, but they can't overcome the taste of the food in this place. If they have cream of portabella mushroom soup, order it. If no other entrees appeal, try the sand dabs, which are covered in capers and vegetables.

The details are impressive, even to the fresh taste of the vinegar mixed in with the dipping oil for bread. And in the mashed potatoes, two crisps stick up like ears. This is a place where you really want the coffee. It's rich.

The dozen entrees are in the $17 to $25 range. For a full dinner — with a starter, entrée, desert and wine, tax and tip — I'd figure about $60 per person. A simpler lunch is maybe $15.

For what it's worth, PortaBella and its adjoining bistro are related to **The Grill on Ocean Avenue** a block up the street, which has a menu and prices similar to PortaBella in a less-cozy setting, and **Anton & Michel Restaurant** on Mission Street, which I simply don't like.

La Boheme on Dolores Street near 7th Avenue in Carmel for the past 20 years, is cozy enough to be a friend's living room, even if it's in a storefront building. It's a jewel of a little restaurant, with indoor awnings and decorated walls to add to the cozy.

The restaurant, which serves dinner only, has maybe a dozen tables but doesn't take reservations. On busy nights, you can see the crowd milling around on the sidewalk out front, waiting to get in.

The restaurant offers a single dinner at a fixed price of $21.75, with meat, seafood and fowl menus set in advance and provided for anyone who calls, stops by or calls up the Web site.

The last dinner I had there was prawns in a tomato sauce. I have to say the prawns were a little rubbery, but the tomato sauce was delightful, the rice and spinach side dishes okay. The best parts of the fixed-price dinner were clearly the first courses — a salad with such a mix of fresh vegetables it just exploded all over my taste buds and a chicken soup that was as good as I always imagine homemade to be.

For dessert, which is $5 extra, I'd recommend sharing a pear soaked in pinot noir. Wow, is that good!

With that and wine, I'd figure the real fixed price at about $50.

Chez Christian is one of those cozy little places you're glad to know about. It sits hidden behind a bunch of stores in a quaint plaza called the Court of the Golden Bough off Ocean Avenue, between Lincoln and Monte Verde streets. You have to walk behind a candy store, a miniature-art store and a tea shop to find it.

Once you're there, the secluded French restaurant lives up to its expectations. The main dining room – dominated by a bay window and mirrors – has only seven tables. The kitchen has room for only one person – Chef Christian, of course.

But there's a good variety of pastas, seafoods, poultries and meats coming from the small kitchen, generally in the $15 to $20 range. I can't fault the generous servings of bay scallops over fettuccini.

Chez Felix is a cute little mom-and-pop restaurant in the corner of Sundial Lodge, right next to City Hall at Monte Verde and 7th Avenue.

It is classic French, no nouvelle cuisine, no tiny portions, no mystery combos. There are lots of mushrooms in the dishes.

The place is charming, white walls and red tablecloths, with seating for maybe 30 people.

And the prices are amazing, about half the going rates in Carmel. There's usually a two-course dinner special for $12.50.

I'd try the crab bisque, the garlic dip and, of course, something with mushrooms.

The Terrace Grill in La Playa Hotel is every bit as classy as the picturesque hotel itself. It just glows with the elegance and taste of old money.

The oak woodwork in the rafters and ceilings is humbling, while the thick walls show the graceful waves formed by skilled and loving hands, the windows look out over the flowers and gardens that have invited countless weddings to the old hotel.

La Playa, which helps set a tone in Carmel, is just a couple of blocks from the beach at 8th Avenue and Camino Real. It is certainly a delightful place to visit.

The food is good, but I'd have to caution that it's not really great. On a five-star system, I'd put in at about three. There is a big menu, including food for the adjoining bar, one of the classics in Carmel. Lunches are sandwiches, salads and pastas in the $10 range. Dinners are meatier and more like $15 to $20. There's a cleaver artichoke ravioli that, at $12, may be the best deal on the menu.

L'Escargot, in a cottage behind a lawyer's office on Mission Street near 4th Avenue, is a friendly cafe with booths and tables that look properly experienced. It's been there more than 40 years and has counted the likes of Elizabeth Taylor as a regular at one time.

The shelves around the walls are filled with a collection of dishes, plates and platters that suggest the owners actually live in this cozy cottage. It's a very relaxing place, except for the French music in the background, which I find irritating.

The food is generally great. No, you don't have to have the namesake snails, especially if you have the same aversions I do. But I'd make sure to have something with wild mushrooms, as the restaurant serves whatever can be found in Big Sur that day.

The other vegetables are pureed and carefully placed on plates in colorful patterns. The bread and pastries are outstanding. And if you're celebrating, the Grand Marnier souffle really can't be beat.

I would easily rank this as one of the very best restaurants in the area, except twice I've had overcooked entrees. Try as I may, I just haven't been able to overlook that.

Simpson's, on the corner of San Carlos Street and 5th Avenue, is a pleasant restaurant that has been in business at the same location for decades. That really says a lot in a place as trendy as Carmel.

The large dining room is relaxing, with space between the tables, bright murals on one wall, windows on the others. It has a solid feel to it, a friendly staff and an appreciative atmosphere that isn't rushed or hurried.

It's a place where you want to try the soups – and you should. They are robust and flavorful. You also want to try the rice and corn cakes, a delightful way to present vegetables. I like the crab cakes, which are huge and crammed full of meat. The portions are large, so keep that in mind if you're heading for dessert.

Village Corner at Dolores Street and 6th Avenue is a pleasant cafe in a wonderfully central location, with an outdoor patio in good weather.

It may be the only place in Carmel that has both paella and porter house on the menu, and a healthy range of dishes in between.

Lunch time offers sandwiches, salads, and pastas for less than $10. Dinner is more like $15-$20.

This may not be the greatest food you're going to have in your life, but for these prices in Carmel it's okay. There are some places around that are simply awful, with a capital A. You have to think expensive for most of the better restaurants in this resort.

Patisserie Boissiere Cafe is a treat in the middle of Carmel. It offers good food — lunch, dinner, or take out — at reasonable prices.

The dining room, inspired by French country, is small and relatively informal. It always reminds me of going into the dining room at an aunt's house, there's that kind of wholesome quality.

Patisserie Boissiere is at the side of the Carmel Plaza, right next to the steps on Mission Street, between Ocean and 7th Avenue.

The fillos are nice. There's also a selection of soup, salads, sandwiches, pastas and pastries. The shepherd's pie is delightful. Lunches are generally under $10, while dinners are a few bucks more.

Flying Fish Grill is tucked away in a corner of the lower level of the Carmel Plaza, near the Mission Street entrance, sort of under Patisserie Boissiere Café.

It's worth looking for because it's an excellent restaurant that provides some of the most unusual food on the Monterey Peninsula. The kitchen uses very inventive blends of Asian, European and California concepts.

I love the salmon there that's cooked in parchment, which I'm told is a French concept. But the Flying Fish cooks it with Chinese black beans and ginger in a fusion that provides a tender, moist salmon filet with a pungent taste. It's wonderful.

Most of the seafood there is delightful, even, I'm told, the rare ahi tuna that's much too rare for my taste.

The restaurant is small and cozy, with high-backed booths providing a feeling of privacy and intrigue. A selection of unusual appetizers are in the $5 to $10 range, while dinners you may not encounter anywhere else are in the $15 to $20 range.

Robata Grill & Sake Bar is on the ground floor of The Barnyard shopping center alongside Highway 1, between Rio and Carmel Valley roads.

It's the granddaddy of good Japanese restaurants here, and it's just as good and just as much fun as it always was.

There are tables under heat lamps on the patio, cozy booths inside, tables in the bar and a counter around the sushi bar, if you want to watch the four sushi chefs work.

Robata certainly has the most varied menu of the Japanese restaurants in the area, making it easy to mix sushi and appetizers to design your own meal. This could be your chance to try raw sea urchin and still have rolled beef, deep-fried vegetables, chicken teriyaki and other things you know you like. Figure $5 to $7 per item.

Lugano Swiss Bistro is just across from Robata, on the ground floor near the back of The Barnyard shopping center at the mouth of Carmel Valley. It provides good, substantial food at good prices, nothing for the faint-hearted or strictly herbal set.

It's heavy on sausages, pork and veal dishes, as you would expect to find in Switzerland. And yes, there's fondue, the real cheese dip that starts around $14 a person. I should note that the homemade pasta — called spatzli — is breadier than the noodles you might be used to, and its' heavy with grease. It's excellent, if your taste buds are bold, and it certainly won't leave you hungry.

This place certainly doesn't hold back on the food. There's a three-sausage platter, for example ($10.50 at lunch, $15.75 at dinner), that could easily feed two people.

But you can do lighter with soups and salads, which seems to be what a lot of the shopping center workers have for lunch.

The restaurant itself is surprisingly cozy, with lots of wood and beer steins suggesting comfort food.

I have to admit that I avoided Lugano's for a long time because it advertises heavily and has discount coupons everywhere. I always consider those signs that there's not much repeat business or word-of-mouth support. But several friends who have become regulars here convinced me that I was wrong. And I was.

Wasabi Bistro is in the middle of The Crossroads shopping center, that chi-chi center at Highway 1 and Rio Road at the mouth of Carmel Valley, down the road from the mission.

This is Japanese food as you might expect it in Japan — lots of sushi with a few cooked entrees on the menu, notably teryaki and tempura in the $9 to $13 range. But those things are also available in appetizer portions so you can have the real fun of the place, the sushi.

The prices vary, but most rolls seem to be $4.50 for six pieces. I especially like shitake mushroom sushi with avocado or tofu, and spicy tuna. I'd figure a couple of rolls, an appetizer and a soup for a meal — $15, plus a few bucks for beer or sake, of course.

There's a large dining room next to a room that has two sushi bars in it. It's open for both lunch and dinner.

The Covey Restaurant at Quail Lodge, a posh golf resort on Carmel Valley Road, has been one of the three or four best restaurants in the area for a long time. It's certainly been one of the most expensive, and still is.

But I was so disappointed the last time I was there I dropped The Covey from the "Very Best" list because I don't think there's a lot of room for disappointment at their prices. I find that it costs at least $80 per person for the works — appetizers, desserts, wine, tax and tips.

I've had meals worth those prices at The Covey in the past, and was delighted to find them using local foods in ways I would never have thought of.

But the last time I was there I found my dinner was pretty pedestrian. The mashed potatoes were the best thing on my plates and that really shouldn't be the test of a kitchen.

I was also served a dessert that night that was so salty it was inedible. The staff acknowledged an error in the kitchen and apologized for it. But, again, at those prices that's inexcusable.

The place itself is still elegant — the kinds of woods and windows money and taste can put together, with lots of linens, silver, comfortable chairs and a view of a fountain in a peaceful duck pond.

PEBBLE BEACH

Roy's at Pebble Beach is the informal restaurant in The Inn at Spanish Bay.

The food is so good and the view is so stunning that this is clearly a candidate for my best list. But the trendy look to the place, the sometimes-rushed service and the fact that this is part of a Hawaii-based chain keeps it off.

The food is great and I wouldn't hesitate to recommend it. It's primarily seafood and it's high-priced – roughly $15 for lunch, about $25 for dinner entrees.

The hibachi-grilled salmon is some of the best-tasting salmon I've ever had, and I've had lots of salmon. There's also a swordfish steak crusted with lemon grass, basil and peanut sauce that'll knock your socks off, if you like spicy fish. And the ravioli filled with shiitake mushrooms will make you wonder why you haven't thought of doing that before.

The view of the surf pounding the wraparound seashore of Spanish Bay is stunning on a sunny day, subdued at night. It says sit for a while and admire, but the service can be so rushed that you get the impression they need the dishes back in a hurry.

10 Restaurants For the View

I've got some favorite restaurants that are favorites because of the spectacular, one-of-a-kind settings they provide in this scenic paradise. Be aware, the food is lousy in some of them. But a view, you might say, is sometimes worth a thousand tastes. Here's my list:

FISHERMAN'S WHARF AREA

Elves Grill and Boat Hoist on Municipal Wharf No. 2 — the shorter one near Fisherman's Wharf — is a little jewel of a diner.

The food isn't that terrific — I always stick to the torpedo burger for lunch, a double cheeseburger with fries for $5.95.

But the location and the ambiance are divine.

This place, named for the family that now owns it, was called Joe's Bait Shop when I used to vacation in Monterey. One of my favorite things on those trips was getting up before dawn so I could get to Joe's for breakfast while the commercial fishermen were in the place. There were those just coming in from a night of pulling nets from the ocean, swapping tales of the sea with those about to go out with boatloads of tourists.

The fishermen are mostly gone now, moved along by a change of ownership and a remodeling that has brightened the place up and put flower boxes around the windows, and cappuccino on the menu.

I haven't been there for breakfast in years, since I live here now and can make decent eggs at home. But I love to pop in at lunchtime for an occasional torpedo burger and fresh breath of the bay.

Sandbar & Grill is sort of underneath the Elves Grill on the small wharf, the one that is officially named Municipal Wharf No. 2, which caters to the commercial fishing fleet of Monterey.

The food isn't that good, but the daytime views are delightful. The restaurant sits under the wharf, so the windows are right next to the piers and the passing boats. There's usually a good show from this place.

At night, the place turns into a piano bar, if you like that sort of thing.

AQUARIUM AREA/CANNERY ROW

The Duck Club Restaurant is on the lower level of the Monterey Plaza, the big, shiny hotel at about the center of Cannery Row.

The restaurant doesn't feature as much duck as you might guess from its name. It has only one duck meal on its menu – the Steinbeck roasted duck dinner for $22. There's a much bigger selection of beef and seafood.

But the place features a mesmerizing view of Monterey Bay — with the kayakers and passing boats in the daytime, the lights of Monterey and Seaside at night. The smokestacks of the Pacific Gas & Electric Co. plant at Moss Landing provide a landmark on the distant shoreline.

You get the same wondrous view from **Schooners Bistro** next door, which serves the lunch The Duck Club doesn't. For a $10 sandwich, you can absorb more elegance than anyone is entitled to.

El Torito Mexican Restaurant and Cantina on Cannery Row and Hoffman Avenue is a chain restaurant that I would never consider recommending in a local guidebook.

But here it is, despite its paint by number menu, because of the view it provides through the windows. It's a terrific Monterey Bay view.

You get the same view with drinks or coffee as you do with the food, of course. And yes, there is a bar with frosty margaritas and warm chips for $4.25.

Paradiso Trattoria & Oyster Bar opens up some real choices on Cannery Row — providing good food with a priceless view of Monterey Bay.

It wraps around the ground floor of the Spindrift Inn at 654 Cannery Row, about in the middle of the main strip.

One door opens onto a counter overlooking the cooks and the kitchen, a bar with some great wines for $5 and $6 a glass and plateaus of tables overlooking Monterey Bay. Another door opens onto the oyster bar, which reaches down to plateaus of tables.

The place overall has a "sit and relax" feeling that can be hard to find on Cannery Row. It also has a "now let's eat" feeling to it. It's a winner, another success of John Pisto, who runs four Monterey restaurants, writes cookbooks and stars on a televised cooking show.

Paradiso has appetizers, $10 pizzas and whole meals that are in the $12 to $19 range. at lunch time, $15 to $22 at dinner time. The oyster bar has $20 crabs, $10 shrimp cocktails and, of course, oysters for about $2 each.

I wouldn't hesitate to recommend a pasta dish here — linguini with clam sauce may be my favorite. It's got fresh linguini, clams still in the shell and more butter in the broth than I have in my refrigerator. One tip: wear a shirt that won't show the splashes.

The Fish Hopper at 700 Cannery Row is in a wonderful setting with a window seat on Monterey Bay, providing a first-class view of nature that never fails to be mesmerizing. Waves splash around and under the restaurant. Sea otters play in the kelp out in the bay.

All the tables are positioned for the incredible view from this place. Enjoy it. But don't get your hopes up for the food. I've been consistently disappointed by the seafood I've tried. I'd stick to chowder or something deep-fried.

The prices aren't bad, $10 to $14 for a meal. But it's the view that's important.

PACIFIC GROVE

Old Bathhouse Restaurant on Lovers Point at 620 Ocean View Blvd. is a classy little place that always seems overpriced to me.

It's one of the more romantic places around, laid out in trolley-car style with lots of dark wood and candles.

And it is in one of the two or three most beautiful settings in the area, with an absolutely hypnotic view that has drawn people to Pacific Grove for more than a century.

But the food isn't up to the $30 dinner prices. It's generally good, but relatively unimaginative and loaded with heavy sauces, cream and butter, the old-fashioned way.

For these prices, I want better food or, at least, lights on the spectacular scenery outside. Of course, if you get there before 6 p.m., you can get the daylight and an "early-bird" dinner for $22.95.

The Tinnery Restaurant is just across the street from the Old Bathhouse, with lots of windows looking out on Lovers Point.

If you really think you'll eat there, look around for one of the discount coupons that seem to be available everywhere.

What I like this place for is the bar, and I've got lots of qualifiers on that. It has one of only three liquor licenses issued in the Methodist-founded city of Pacific Grove, and one of the other two is used in a little bar squished into the center of a restaurant. When I want a quick drink near my home, this has to be it.

It also serves food late at night, so I sometimes get the $8 cheeseburger or the $7 calamari strips in the bar, after other places have closed. There is also a huge window looking out on a beautiful section of Monterey Bay. The view is divine in daylight or at night, in fog or rain.

CARMEL

Mission Ranch Restaurant is on a winding road directly behind the Carmel Mission at 26270 Dolores St. It offers the very best view from any restaurant in the area, so I recommend going in daylight or, for a great memory, at sunset.

This is the place saved from demolition and still owned and frequented by Clint Eastwood. When the movie star is home in Pebble Beach, he frequently eats dinner here — a vegetarian's potatoes and salads, that I've seen. But I've found the food disappointing, so I almost always stick with beef or go for the $18.95 Sunday brunch. The brunch is good, a bargain at the price. The Ranch has lunch only on Saturdays. Sometimes I just have drinks at the Mission Ranch before — or after — having dinner somewhere else.

You go to this place for the scenery and the considerable ambience. And you go back again and again.

If you hit a clear, windless day when the sun is out and you can get a patio table, it wouldn't matter if they served burned oatmeal. It's delightful.

It's the only place in the world you can watch sheep grazing in the meadow behind the restaurant, framed on one side by the river flowing into Carmel Bay, on another by the surf licking at the beach where people and dogs are playing. In the distance is Point Lobos, the cove-loaded outcropping that Robert Louis Stevenson used as his setting for "Treasure Island."

BIG SUR

Nepenthe on Highway 1, just south of Ventana, is a legendary stop on the Big Sur coast, once a retreat for the Hollywood elite.

Now it's a restaurant that features a hamburger called "the famous ambrosiaburger." It's priced at $10.75.

There is a variety of other sandwiches in that price range, soups and salads. But what you really get at Nepenthe is food for the spirit.

The restaurant sits in the crisp air among treetops at the top of a cliff, overlooking a mesmerizing view of the Pacific coast. The coastline at Nepenthe is that gorgeous one that has huge, humpback, forlorn rocks that jut out into the ocean like fingers on a hand. There are frequently layers of fog over and around them, shrouding them in mystery. On the shoreline below the restaurant, there are stands of tall pines, broken by meadows that cry out for sheep.

Birds flutter through the treetops, whistling and singing. If you sit at the tables on the patio, some of the birds may join you.

Nepenthe opens at 11:30 a.m. If you want something earlier — or at a slightly lower level — there is **Cafe Kevah** just down the steps from Nepenthe. It opens at 9 a.m. and offers omelettes, waffles, soups, salads and pies – in the $5-$12 range.

The 10 or 11 Very Best Restaurants

If you're going to drop $100 on dinner, it might as well be good.

There are lots of places in the Monterey Peninsula-Carmel area where you can easily spend that kind of money for dinner with or without wine.

Some of them are actually worth it.

Most aren't.

I feel suckered at pricey restaurants where the food is mediocre, the servings notably small, the tables jammed together, or the service rude.

But I've found 10 or 11 here that are consistently worth the higher prices, relaxing and fun places that provide good food and dining memories you can count on.

You've got to hurry for the 11th, though. **Gernot's Victoria House Restaurant** near the post office in downtown Pacific Grove, one of my absolute favorites, is for sale as this edition goes to press. But it would be worth calling 646-1477 to see if it's still open, if Gernot is still cooking and if you can get a table in its European elegance.

Now here are the 10 longer-term restaurants I consider the very best in the area, the places I wish I could afford to eat at more often:

Stokes Adobe Restaurant at 500 Hartnell St., a block from Monterey City Hall, has quickly become one of my No. 1 eateries.

It's in a great, 160-year-old building that for decades housed Gallatin's, the most highly rated restaurant between San Francisco and Los Angeles. The adobe has housed a lot of restaurants in the decade since Gallatin's closed, but the present one is clearly the best.

I've had about half the items on the menu and not one of them has been weak, routine or less than spectacular. This place has some of the best food I've ever found here.

They make wonderful sausage, ravioli that melts in your mouth, duckling in beans you wouldn't believe and roasted pork chops that are packaged with bread pudding and fruit picked from the trees out front.

Once I found pound cake with polenta mixed in, covered by lemon sauce, that was worth the trip to town.

And it's not the most expensive food I've found. Entrees are in the $15 to $20 range. With an appetizer, dessert, wine, tax and tip, I'd figure about $55 per person for dinner, about $15 for a simpler lunch.

The main dining room can be noisy. But what the hell, drink more wine and talk louder, like I do.

Fresh Cream Restaurant near Fisherman's Wharf in Monterey is touted as one of the very best in the area, if not the very best.

It is excellent, with an elegance to it that you might expect in a classy French restaurant.

Clearly it is one of the best restaurants here, but Fresh Cream is just a little bit stuffy for my taste.

It sits on the second floor of 100C Heritage Harbor, overlooking the Monterey Bay Recreation Trail, Fisherman's Wharf and the harbor.

The place is spacious, as restaurants in resort areas go. It's divided into three dining rooms — one with windows overlooking the scenery, the other two with old Monterey paintings on the walls and lots of flowers and linen to make them relaxing.

The staff, some in tuxedos, is very attentive without being pretentious.

And the food is excellent. The salads are fresh and not soaked in oil, the cooked vegetables are crisp, the puff pastry is just where it's needed, the entrees are pretty and the desserts are terrific.

I wouldn't hesitate to recommend the duck in black currant sauce. I'm also a sucker for good ravioli with fresh crab in them, like Fresh Cream sometimes offers.

For dessert, you can't go wrong with the vanilla cream.

With a local wine, I'd figure about $75 per person for dinner.

Monterey's Fish House at 2114 Del Monte Ave. in Monterey is an unpretentious cafe that serves seafood the way it's supposed to be – fresh, prepared with attention and imagination, presented in huge portions.

The place, a former hamburger stand with bad acoustics, is about a half-mile from downtown Monterey. It was taken over a few years ago by a collection from old Monterey fishing families and French restaurant chefs. They have turned it into the essence of Monterey – outstanding food in a casual setting that could be Aunt Theresa's kitchen.

Pastas start around $9, specials are in the $15 range. The ravioli filled with crab may be my favorite dish. The cioppino is clearly the best in the area – meaty, with tomato sauce that calls for more bread for soaking. And Monterey prawns, during their short season, are delightful.

With salad, wine, coffee, tax and tip, I'd figure about $35 per person, and I'd expect to be hungry again in about a week.

Raffaello Carmel Restaurant is on Mission Street, just south of Ocean Avenue (Carmel doesn't have street numbers), sort of across the street from the Carmel Plaza shopping center.

Without a doubt, this is the best Italian food in the Monterey Peninsula-Carmel area. But it's not cheap. I figure more than $50 a person (including antipasto, mousse, wine, tax and tip), so it's a good place to take people when we're on *their* expense accounts. The sauces are heavy and creamy and rich, none of this watery, runny stuff served in more modern restaurants. The ravioli and pastas are superb.

Unlike most Carmel restaurants, this one is fairly spacious, so you can have conversations at your dinner table that are as quiet, romantic and private as you care to make them.

Casanova, on 5th Avenue between Junipero and San Carlos, is one of those cozy places with great food that makes Carmel memorable.

It is pricey, with almost nothing on the dinner menu under $30. In fact, Casanova has gone to a three-course dinner where you choose only the main course, generally in the $30 to $35 price range. Lunches you can do for half that.

But it is a delightful treat. If it's not raining, I'd recommend the patio instead of one of the small dining rooms. It's mostly enclosed, with a plastic roof and awnings that let the tree grow through. There are some gorgeous tiles creating floral arrangements and fruit bowls on the thick stucco walls.

It has those heat lamps that warm the night. The candlelight is dim, designed for romance and conversation, not reading. And the dress is about as casual as anyone wants it to be.

The place is wonderful, the food inventive. I figure about $75 per person for dinner.

Rio Grill is in The Crossroads shopping center just outside Carmel near the intersection of Highway 1 and Rio Road.

This was my favorite restaurant here, but the noise in the place bothers me as I get older. I considered dropping it from my Very Best list, but the food is just so damned good, I can't.

I can rarely get out for less than $50 a person but the food is usually superb. When there's fresh Monterey Bay salmon cooked in parchment in the summer, it is the best meal in town. When the specials don't appeal to me, I usually fall back on a chicken cooked in chili butter, which is served on a bed of baby potatoes and artichokes. Occasionally I'll have liver, which is crispy and flavorful and unlike any I've ever had before.

The only thing I really avoid at the Rio is pasta because it's been mediocre in the past.

On the bad side, the Rio Grill is usually crowded and, like I said, noisy, making it a difficult place for a quiet, romantic conversation. Reservations are crowded together too, so your table is rarely ready on time and you're not encouraged to linger over a second cup of coffee.

Robert Kincaid's Bistro is one of the restaurants clustering in The Crossroads shopping center at Highway 1 and Rio Road, just outside Carmel.

It is clearly one of the best and most inviting restaurants in the area. But it is hardly the first French restaurant for Kincaid, who originated Fresh Cream in Monterey years ago.

This restaurant is a charming collection of rooms, fireplaces and booths. It's relatively informal, with shirtsleeves at dinner a common sight.

I didn't think I liked sea scallops until one night at Kincaid's. A stranger at the next table said he'd pay the bill if I didn't like them there. It turned out to be a safe offer. The scallops were divine – a generous serving with a red pepper sauce, a dill sauce and a butter sauce. The vegetables on the side couldn't have been better. Even the rice seemed better than rice.

Dinners are generally in the $25 range, appetizers and desserts generally $6-$7. I figure $60 per person for the full treatment.

Lunch is a fixed-price, three-course, French meal for $16.

Stillwater Bar & Grill is proof that the Pebble Beach folks know how to make a restaurant.

This place is classy without being pretentious. It's got tables and comfortable chairs lined up along windows that look out on an extraordinarily beautiful view of the ocean, the shoreline and the much-televised 18th hole of the world-famous Pebble Beach Golf Links.

The view is really unbeatable, a vista that sweeps over Stillwater Cove, the white sand of Carmel Beach and the tree-shrouded cottages up the hillside from it, the Santa Lucia Mountains across the bay and the poetic Point Lobos. The white caps of the surf are mesmerizing as they crash against the rocks.

The food is superb, too. Versions of seafood dominate the menu, of course — as entrees, salads, soups, sandwiches, ravioli and hors d'oeuvres. A dozen oysters, with your pick from at least four kinds, can start you off for $16 a dozen. The main courses for lunch from about $10 to $18, dinners from $20 to $27, unless you're having the $52 abalone. For the works, without abalone, I'd figure about $60 per person for dinner,

$25 for lunch.

I'd order the seafood ravioli, if it's on the menu. I had it one time with salmon, tuna and sea bass blended into pastas as big as burritos, covered in a cream sauce so rich it should have made me feel guilty. There was bread mixed in with the dish, for diners too polite to lick their plates in public, I guess.

The Stillwater is one of the main restaurants in the elegant Lodge at Pebble Beach. It's on the main floor of the hotel, right off the lounge area that's filled with comfortable sofas, music and sparkling-clean windows looking out on that amazing view.

The other main restaurant at The Lodge is **Club XIX**, which sits below on the ground floor. It's more famous and more expensive (a hamburger for lunch, for example, is $12.50), with some seafood on the menu, along with the beef dishes, lamb and venison. The place did recently loosen its long-standing dress code that required men to wear jackets for dinner; they are now suggested, but not required. Still, I'd stay upstairs.

Pacific's Edge Restaurant is the elegant restaurant at the Highlands Inn, about 10 miles south of Carmel on Highway 1.

It has a simpler sister next door, **The California Market**.

Both provide great food and mesmerizing views of the ocean.

Pacific's Edge is a classy place that recently served dinner to the president and regularly hosts banquets and conferences for gourmets, chefs and winemakers most of us have heard of. Fortunately it serves the rest of us , too.

I prefer the place for lunch — or the Sunday brunch — to take full advantage of the setting. Nights might be more romantic, but the view is restricted so you can't see the tops of the pines around you, the white caps cascading off the rocks below you, the animals on Pelican Point at the edge of Point Lobos State Reserve next door, the hills of Carmel Bay, the clouds that float in the sky.

You're not likely to be disappointed by the food at any meal. You may even want to lick the plate to make sure you get it all.

And if the food and the view weren't enough to convince me this place is worth the price, I would be won over by the fact that the house wine is Chalone. Chalone is one of the most celebrated wineries in Monterey County, with a limited output that makes it hard to find in stores.

I figure about $40 per person for a leisurely lunch, $50 for the Sunday brunch and $85 for dinner at this Mobil four-star restaurant. There is a fixed-price option, full dinners for $56 a person, or choices of inventive appetizers for about $12 each, entres for about $40.

The California Market next door is a more casual setting with a sim-

43

pler menu. But the quality will knock your socks off.

There is a patio/balcony/terrace/deck with a dozen tables in the fresh air. At sunsets and in the evenings, the electric heaters help. There are also tables inside, some by windows that overlook the stunning view, some by a fireplace.

The wine is the same — Chalone chardonnay or pinot noir for about $8 a glass. I think the most expensive dish is the Atlantic salmon on white beans for $15, while sandwiches, pizzas and quesadillas in the $10 range dominate the menu. If they happen to have carrot soup while you're there, treat yourself to an amazing use of a vegetable.

The Ventana Inn is in Big Sur, about a half-hour south of Carmel on Highway 1. The drive is breathtaking, winding along cliffs over the ocean and cutting through redwood groves.

This is one of my alltime favorite brunch places. The morning drive along the Big Sur coast is a world-class event, the ocean and mountain views from Ventana's outdoor dining area is spellbinding, the blue jays that steal sugar packages off your table are entertaining and the food is excellent.

I figure about $25 a person for the eggs Benedict on weekends or lunch (without wine or extras, tax and tip included), which I think is a real bargain for the luxuriousness of it.

At dinner time there's now a fixed-price option – $39 for three courses, $49 for four. I'm willing to try anything on the Ventana menu. I don't believe I've ever been disappointed.

The only bad side is that you really shouldn't drink before you face the drive back on a winding, busy highway. But, then, the food and scenery provide a mellow intoxication of their own.

For dinner, well, it's best if you can stay overnight in the luxury hotel at Ventana. You don't have to face that winding highway at night and the hotel is an adventure in pampering. I figure about $70 per person for dinner, $300 for the room.

THOM'S
GUIDE
TO
GOOD
EATING
on the
Peninsula...

10 Ready-made Picnics

If you haven't seen an ideal picnic spot yet, check some of the other sections of this book for suggestions.

When you're ready to try one, you can get the old cheese and crackers for lunch, or maybe some trail mix, or a bag of burgers or take-out chicken from one of the chain outlets here.

But if you want a good sandwich and some salads, chips, drinks and even desserts to go with them, here's a list of the places near good spots that have ready-made picnics.

Monte Vista Market is in the vicinity of Del Monte Shopping Center in Monterey. It's at 15 Soledad Drive, about two blocks west of the shopping center, three blocks from the Munras Avenue exit of Highway 1. It's a full grocery store that has anything you want to go, with the biggest $5 sandwiches in the area. I'd take one of their lunches anywhere, but maybe Jacks Peak near the airport would be the closest spot of pure wonder.

Troia's Market is near the Monterey waterfront. It sits at Pacific Street and Del Monte Avenue, just across from the Marriott and the DoubleTree. The best thing about Troia's is its location. The sandwiches are okay, but it's the proximity that makes this place recommended — the waterfront or, if you're in a more floral mood, a neat, little park named Friendly Plaza that's two blocks down Pacific Street at the Monterey City Hall complex.

Valnizza's Market at 401 Ocean Ave. in Monterey is a little harder to find, but worth the effort. It's in a residential area near the Naval Postgraduate School and offers huge, hot or cold sandwiches for $4 to $5. You can use the map at the front of this book to help you get there. It's two blocks north of Camino Aguajito, the northern border of marvelous El Estero Park. Fourth Street up two blocks to Ocean Avenue, or go up Del Monte Avenue for two blocks, turn right onto Ocean and go four more.

Bagel Bakery has stores in Monterey, Pacific Grove, Carmel and Sand City. They offer the best and freshest bagels in the area, and they also use them as rolls to make sandwiches that are suitable for picnics. The most expensive is about $4, a turkey and cranberry combination that mushes all over your hands.

One of the stores in Monterey is at 201 Lighthouse Ave., just two blocks up from Cannery Row, across from the Coast Guard station, midway between Fisherman's Wharf and the Monterey Bay Aquarium. There are lots of picnic places along the waterfront near that store, including a grassy park, sandy beaches and a wooden pier.

The other Bagel Bakeries are downtown at 452 Alvarado St., in Pacific Grove at 1132 Forest Ave., at the mouth of Carmel Valley at 26539 Carmel Rancho Blvd. and in Sand City in the Borders-Circuit City-Target shopping center alongside Highway 1.

Goodies is a deli in Pacific Grove that some of my friends like a lot better than I do. But it's in a good location if you want to pick up a picnic for Lovers Point or any of the other parks, beaches or pullouts along the town's mesmerizing shoreline. The deli is downtown at 518 Lighthouse Ave. and offers a complete line of sandwiches for $5 or $6, salads, soups and terrific dill pickles.

Pebble Beach Market has **two stores**, one across from the famous Lodge at Pebble Beach at the heart of the 17-Mile Drive, the other at the Pacific Grove gate on Sunset Drive, near Asilomar. Both are well-stocked with sandwich and picnic ingredients, good selections of wines and other drinks to take along. There are picnic tables behind the markets. Other spots can be found all along 17-Mile Drive on accessible beaches, in groves of trees and on grassy slopes. Near the Pacific Grove gate there's a section of the Del Monte Forest, Asilomar State Beach and a table-laden beach at Spanish Bay.

Mediterranean Market is in downtown Carmel, at the corner of Ocean Avneue and Mission Street. It's got a complete delicatessen that allows any combination of things you can think of. And it's got a wine section worth browsing through. Luckily, the Mediterranean sits just across the street from the city's Devendorf Park, a grassy reprieve that offers benches, people watching and sometimes music. If you don't want to eat in that park, there's another one on a hill with a scenic overlook about a half-mile up Junipero Avenue. Or there's the white sand beach about a half-mile down Ocean Avenue.

Bruno's Market in Carmel is sort of catty-cornered from Devendorf Park at the corner of Junipero and 6th avenues. It's a full grocery store with ready-mades in the deli, sandwiches made to order, a good produce section and a delightful selection of local wines.

Neilsen Brothers Market at San Carlos Street and 7th Avenue is the third Carmel stop for ready-made picnics. It's also a full grocery with one of the best wine selections in the area. Keep your eyes open for Clint Eastwood, who is a regular customer here.

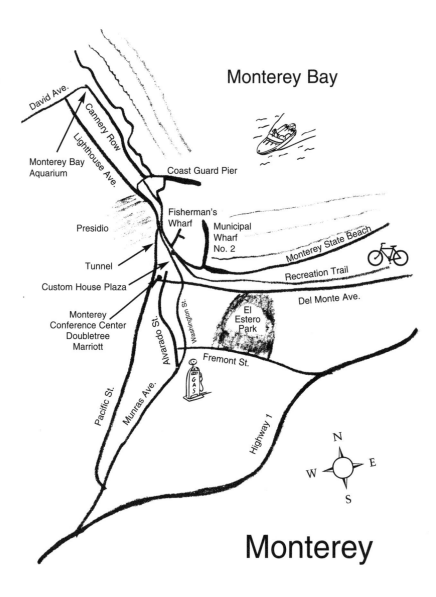

Monterey Bay

David Ave.

Cannery Row

Lighthouse Ave.

Monterey Bay
Aquarium

Coast Guard Pier

Presidio

Fisherman's
Wharf

Municipal
Wharf
No. 2

Monterey State Beach

Tunnel

Recreation Trail

Custom House Plaza

Del Monte Ave.

Monterey
Conference Center
Doubletree
Marriott

Washington St.

El
Estero
Park

Alvarado St.

Fremont St.

GAS

Pacific St.

Munras Ave.

Highway 1

N

W ←→ E

S

Monterey

Monterey:
Where History Began

We might as well begin at the beginning in Monterey, down near Fisherman's Wharf, where the first boat is known to have landed nearly 400 years ago.

Stand near the foot of the wharf, in front of the 1827-vintage Custom House and the new Maritime Museum of Monterey. That's about the spot where Sebastian Vizcaino landed in 1602 while looking for harbors for Spanish galleon. He named the place "Monterey" as a new world namesake of the Spanish Count of Monterey.

The actual landing site has been filled in and paved over since then, so that we might stand on it without getting our feet wet.

But from that spot you can look south (that's AWAY from the water) a half-mile or so and see the graceful arch of the oldest building in Monterey — the Royal Presidio Chapel that is now the main sanctuary of San Carlos Catholic Church, built in 1794 to replace the burnt mission Father Junipero Serra built on the site in 1770.

You can look north and see the wharf, which still accommodates a few fishing boats among the sight-seeing excursions, restaurants and carmel-corn stands geared to today's important tourist industry. The paved strip to the left of the wharf is the Monterey Bay Recreation Trail, a bike, running and walking trail that stretches 2 1/2 miles from this spot and passes the Monterey harbor, Cannery Row and an ocean preserve along a rocky coastline to get to Lovers Point in Pacific Grove.

To the east of the Vizcaino landing site is the marina, with the masts of a couple hundred boats cutting patterns in the sky. On the backside of the marina is Municipal Wharf No. 2, where the commercial fishing boats unload their catches of salmon, rock cod and squid for local dinners.

To the immediate west is the Custom House, a structure built for tax collecting when Monterey was the capital of the Mexican province of Alta California. It is the oldest government building in Monterey.

In the distance behind the Custom House is the grassy slope of the Presidio of Monterey, the original Army post that now houses the Defense Language School.

Immediately behind the Custom House is a plaza where you can frequently see fishing nets stretched out to be mended, friendly boccie ball games, summer shows and occasional crafts fairs. On the other side of the plaza is the Doubletree Hotel, which is attached to the Monterey Conference Center.

Beyond that is downtown Monterey, a relatively small area built generally around Alvarado Street, which has recently become a lively collection of coffeehouses, restaurants and nightclubs.

If you want a walking tour of the historic buildings in the area — including the first wood building, built in 1844; the first brick house, built in 1847; the first public building in California, the birthplace of the state Constitution, Colton Hall, which was built from Monterey shale after the Americans occupied California in 1846; a small adobe house where Nobel Prize-winning author John Steinbeck lived for a few years; and a half-dozen other adobes that date back to the 1820s — step into the information booth the state Department of Parks and Recreation maintains in the lobby of the Maritime Museum and sign up.

The 80-minute guided tour is $5. Admission to the Maritime Museum is $3. And there is a free movie that condenses the history of Monterey to 14 minutes without glossing over the destruction of the Indians who lived here for at least 2,000 years before the Spanish took over.

THINGS TO DO

There are lots of things to do in Monterey, many of them from the Fisherman's Wharf area.

For example, there are glass-bottom boats that offer tours of the harbor for $6, fishing boats that cruise along Cannery Row for $10 and a sail boat that offers $35 rides on Monterey Bay.

In season, which usually peaks in late December and early January, there are $15 whale-watching trips available on the fishing fleet anchored at the wharf. When the water is calm, this is one of the best buys in Monterey, a two-hour cruise of the bay with a chance to see lots of those majestic sea creatures close-up.

There are also deep-sea fishing trips available from the four fishing companies at the wharf. They start around 6 a.m. each day and range from about $30 to $125, depending on the day and the season, plus licenses, tackle and bait.

You can also rent bikes by the hour, skates, mopeds, roadster replicas, kayaks, boats and scuba diving equipment in Monterey.

But I never get enough of just walking, standing and looking. I swear, I can stand at Fisherman's Wharf for hours just absorbing sunshine and watching boats come and go, staring at sea otters frolicking and feeding in the marina, listening to the sea lions bark and studying the gulls and pelicans that soar over the water. It's mesmerizing, no matter how many times you've done it.

There are plenty of snack shops and restaurants in the area. (SEE THE LISTS FOR MY FAVORITES.) Souvenirs range from 20-cent postcards to $45 replicas of East Coast lighthouses.

Parking in the city-owned lots at the wharf is a maximum of $8 a day, which is much cheaper than the tickets that pepper the timed parking places on the streets.

MOVING AROUND

If you venture from the Fisherman's Wharf area, the smooth recreation trail alongside Monterey Bay is an invitation for an invigorating walk to Cannery Row, which is less than a mile away.

Cannery Row, which stretches eight or 10 blocks from the Coast Guard Pier to the Monterey Bay Aquarium, now offers T-shirts and tacky souvenirs, bars and restaurants and nightclubs and the rightfully-famous aquarium in the big buildings that used to house sardine canneries.

The walk to the row and past it another mile to Lovers Point in Pacific Grove provides some spectacular views of Monterey Bay, all for free. Remember to bring your camera.

Just across Del Monte Avenue from the wharf is the Monterey Sports Center, where you can swim or work out on modern gym equipment. Behind the sports center are city tennis courts, which are lighted at night.

And if you have children along, a stop at Dennis the Menace Park in the city's El Estero Park is a must. It's right behind the city's tourist-information center, generally across from the wharf. The play-til-you-drop park was a gift to the city from Hank Ketcham, a local resident who created the Dennis the Menace cartoons.

Pacific Grove:
The Sanctuary City

I've come to consider Pacific Grove "the sanctuary city," partly because I live there, partly because it sits along a gorgeous, rocky, five-mile stretch of the Monterey Bay National Marine Sanctuary.

I believe "the grove," as it's sometimes called, has the most varied, accessible and unobstructed shoreline on the Monterey Peninsula, offering beaches, tidepools, walking trails, bicycle trails, scuba diving sites and surfboarding areas for free to anyone who parks along the waterfront. There aren't a lot of picnic tables and public toilets outside of Lovers Point Park, but, hey, nothing's perfect.

The grove is unique on the Monterey Peninsula in that it's the only community that functions as an old-fashioned town, with a downtown shopping district that sells more groceries than T-shirts, residential areas that have eclectic housing designs and kids playing in the streets, public schools and churches scattered around the neighborhoods, gasoline stations where you need them, three hardware stores, a lumber yard and a four-screen movie theater.

It calls itself "The Last Hometown" and it provides the basic services for the 16,000 or so people who live in the grove and the 5,000 or so who live in neighboring Pebble Beach.

Point Pinos, the "Point of Pines," sits right about in the middle of the city's shoreline, marking the southern tip of Monterey Bay as it reaches in from the open Pacific Ocean.

A classic lighthouse stands at that point, a structure built in 1855 that has endured to become the oldest, continuously operated lighthouse on the West Coast. Now maintained by the Pacific Grove Museum of Natural History, the lighthouse is open to the public from 1 to 4 p.m. Thursdays through Sundays.

In addition to the marine sanctuary, Pacific Grove also boasts a monarch butterfly sanctuary, a small, forested section of Ridge Road that the taxpayers decided to buy a few years ago so it wouldn't be developed.

The orange-and-black monarchs — the only insects known to migrate annually — collect in the trees from as far as 2,000 miles away in order to spend winters in the Monterey pines and the tall eucalyptus that shelter them from the cold and winds.

Visiting monarchs are sometimes found in nearby George Washington Park and the El Carmelo Cemetery too, as those trees were part of the same forest before we started cutting down the trees for homesites, motels and so on.

The monarchs can provide one of nature's most dazzling shows. When they are clustered, the butterflies are brown and hang down from the trees like dead leaves or large pine cones. But on a warm afternoon when they break out to feed, the clusters open in a majestic curtain of orange and black that flutters away through the trees. It is a sight worth standing and waiting for.

And if you happen to be there in early October, ask about the butterfly parade, a charming Saturday morning event in which hundreds of school kids dress up in butterfly costumes and parade through downtown to welcome the monarchs back for the winter.

There's another, equally charming event in the grove each year. If you happen to be around in late July, watch for the Feast of Lanterns and, particularly, the Saturday night pageant at Lovers Point. The story enacted year after year tells how young Chinese lovers, fleeing an incensed father, turned themselves into monarchs and flew to Pacific Grove to become the city's first butterflies. It's delightful.

The grove also has some of the most charming bed-and-breakfast inns on the peninsula and about 1,000 motel rooms for tourists. I'm partial to the 7 Gables Inn near Lovers Point, especially the way it's so beautifully lighted at night.

The grove also has some of the most popular, reasonably-priced restaurants in the area, (SEE THE LISTS FOR MY FAVORITES) coffeehouses, art galleries, antique stores, auction houses, a huge outlet center and the only municipal golf course on the peninsula.

The city started in 1875 as a Methodist retreat for San Franciscans who gathered for annual revivals at Lovers Point. It is famed today for its Victorian houses, the oldest of which date back to the 1870s.

There are about 400 cottages still standing in the grove that started as tents for the Methodist retreat. One-inch thick boards were simply nailed around the tents to convert them to cottages suitable for winter. A few of the little houses still have canvas interiors, but most have had drywall added along with foundations, electrical wiring and modern plumbing.

The Heritage Society of Pacific Grove arranges tours of selected Victorians each year. The society also places the green plaques on the fronts of houses that are at least 75 years old and show unique architectural features.

53

Pacific Grove

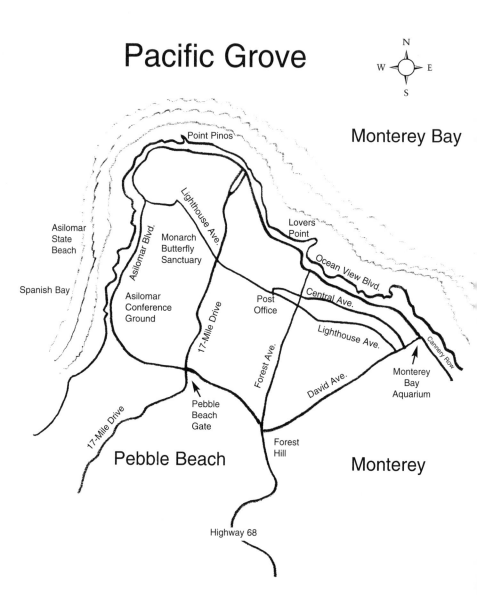

N
W · E
S

Monterey Bay

Point Pinos

Lighthouse Ave.

Asilomar
State
Beach

Asilomar Blvd.

Monarch
Butterfly
Sanctuary

Lovers
Point

Ocean View Blvd.

Spanish Bay

Asilomar
Conference
Ground

17-Mile Drive

Post
Office

Central Ave.

Lighthouse Ave.

Forest Ave.

Cannery Row

David Ave.

Monterey
Bay
Aquarium

17-Mile Drive

Pebble
Beach
Gate

Pebble Beach

Forest
Hill

Monterey

Highway 68

Pebble Beach: The Famous Drive

Pebble Beach is a must at least once in a lifetime.

The spellbinding 17-Mile Drive, which costs $7.50 to get on, stretches along some of the most beautiful shoreline in the world.

There are rocky outcroppings, cliffs, wind-swept cypress trees, the roaring surf and waves crashing into sprays of salty mist.

There are sea gulls and pelicans and cormorants on the rocks off shore, as well as speckled harbor seals and barking sea lions.

There are also golf courses all along the way, with deer munching grass right in among the golfers.

And there are a couple hundred mansions in Pebble Beach, once the playground of the rich and famous from Hollywood. The mansions are now more likely to be owned by corporations, Salinas Valley farmers, oil-rich Arabs and Japanese businessmen. There are also 2,500 other houses in Pebble Beach, many of them in standard subdivisions off the scenic route.

The amazing stuff stretches all along 17-Mile Drive, an historic name for a roadway that now meanders about 10 miles between Pacific Grove and Carmel. The privately-owned road has five gates, where you pay admission and get a map.

The oceanside, mansion-dotted road can be driven in about 30 minutes, but I recommend that you take much longer.

Stop often and feel the wind, watch the surf and study the animals. Walk along the coastal trail if you have time. Head onto a beach and get some sand in your toes and cold water on your feet. The foul smell you sometimes encounter is usually nothing more than rotting seaweed.

Stop at the famous Lone Cypress and try to figure out what has kept that tree alive all these decades. Stop at Cypress Point if it's not closed for the winter seal pupping season and see if you can spot the house Clint Eastwood used in his movie, "Play Misty for Me." Stop at Pescadero Point, if it's not closed by high waves, and look at some of the most turbulent surf in the area. Stop at the 1914-vintage Lodge and look at the posh outfittings and the prices in the shops.

Carmel:
Bring Your Own Parking

Carmel is one of the best-known resorts in the world and if you give it some time, you'll see why.

It is a magical setting, basically on a hillside that slopes down to pristine Carmel Bay and the blue Pacific. There are trees everywhere — big pines and cypress trees that stand as huge umbrellas, gnarled oaks that present fascinating forms. The Pacific at the foot of the hill is buffered by white sand beaches. The rocky lines of Point Lobos sit across the bay.

The setting — along with the cool, foggy Monterey Peninsula climate — is what I've always liked best about Carmel.

The traffic can be discouraging, especially in the summer and on weekends. Remember that this is a one-mile-square village that grew around narrow, winding streets never intended to host the millions of tourists who visit each year. When it's crowded, traffic crawls along and drivers must constantly watch for the many pedestrians and obscure cross streets. It all adds to the carnival atmosphere of tourist season.

Parking is a problem too. A lot of it in the downtown area — the 12 blocks between Junipero and Lincoln Streets, 5th to 7th Avenues — is limited to an enforced 90 minutes or less, just long enough for lunch or a quick round of browsing. Even with those limits, parking spaces can be hard to find.

Carmel really works best when you stay overnight in one of the 993 rental rooms and leave your car in an inn's parking lot.

Then you can explore the 70 or so art galleries at your leisure and sample the 60 restaurants, many of them deservedly famous.

Regardless of how much time you have, browsing — or shopping, if you can afford it — is one of the most popular attractions in Carmel.

There really is some interesting art for sale in this resort that started early in the century as an artists' colony. There's also a lot of schlock that seems to be priced by the square-foot and sold for its color coordination.

Carmel, I believe, really proves the point that one man's art is another man's joke.

I recommend being patient and maintaining a sense of humor when browsing through today's art galleries in Carmel.

Of course, I offer the same advice for browsing through shops anywhere, just more so for the Carmel art galleries.

Watch for the courtyards and alleys off the main blocks and check some of them out. They add to the European charm of the city.

Look for interesting restaurants, bars and coffeehouses while you're downtown. There are a number of good places for breakfast, lunch, dinner or drinks. (SEE THE LISTS FOR MY FAVORITES.)

When you've had enough browsing, capitalism and nutrition, there are lots of free places to check out in Carmel.

TOURING

Take a look at some of the tree-shrouded streets of houses. There is a wide range of architecture in this urban forest, with plenty of shacky cottages and lots of charming little places that look like they came straight out of a fairy tale. Keep in mind that the cheapest place in Carmel sells for about $400,000 these days. And when you see some of the newest, bulky, economic-reality houses, remember that money doesn't buy taste.

Carmel doesn't assign numbers to its houses, so some places are known by unique names, while others are located as "the east side of Lincoln, the third house north of 9th Avenue."

The houses of Carmel are easy to get to. Just head out any street from the downtown area. It's pleasant walking or driving. I might head up 5th Avenue or down Dolores Street, but any residential area in the village can be interesting.

For the grand tour, head to the bottom of Ocean Avenue and let the white sand beach invite you to stretch your legs for a while. Feel free to walk it if you want, wade into the cold water and take lots of pictures. Dogs are also welcome on the Carmel beach.

One of the common photos in Carmel is the city beach, framed by the wind-swept cypress trees that grow at the bottom of Ocean Avenue.

In the car, head down Scenic Road, which is the oceanside drive that starts near the beach and winds around Carmel Point to end near the Carmel Mission.

The mission is well worth a visit. It dates back to 1771 and fuels Catholics with the pioneering spirit of Father Junipero Serra, while it reminds Indians of their days of slavery. The building itself is beautiful, aging adobe walls that have cracked and chipped with such character you could use several rolls of film here.

The church holds Serra's grave, if you're a pilgrim. It functions as a working church, if you're looking for a unique place for Mass.

The mission is on Rio Road, about a half-mile west of Highway 1. Right behind, in the residential area along Lasuen Drive, sits the hotel/bar/restaurant resort named Mission Ranch.

The Mission Ranch is notable for two reasons — it's owned and frequented by Clint Eastwood, who bought the landmark in the 1980s to keep it from being torn down for condominiums; and it provides one of the most spectacular views in the area.

Oh, yeah, Clint is no longer the mayor. He held that office from 1986 to 1988, but you'll still hear tourists ask about "his honor." And you'll still find shops that sell "Clint for mayor" buttons.

If you should happen to run into him while you're here, you'll find he is a truly charming fellow who acts like the guy next door, which, of course, he is when he's here.

THINGS TO DO

If you've got the time and you're looking for something more, here are some other neat things to do in Carmel:

Check the local newspaper listings to see if there's a play at the Forest Theater, which can be a memorable experience.

Check the performance schedule for Sunset Cultural Center, which hosts concerts, music festivals, lectures and meetings. The annual Bach Festival is in July.

In October there is a noted sand castle contest on Carmel Beach.

And yearround there are a variety of playhouses and performance halls. Pacific Repertory Theatre is the most active.

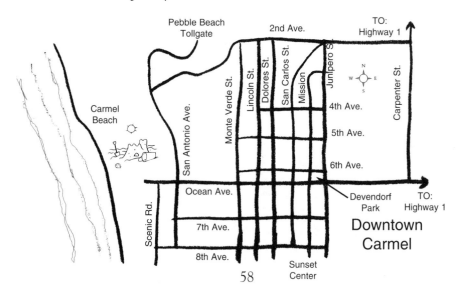

58

Big Sur: Far Out

Big Sur offers one of the most beautiful and unspoiled coastlines in the world, a natural treasure that now has special protections from the federal, state and county governments.

It is a rocky coastline with granite cliffs that stop abruptly for mysterious coves and sandy beaches. There are rocky points that shoot out like fingers, helping break the ocean into a rippling surf that smashes white foam onto the shore and sprays mist into the cool air.

The views from Highway 1 are stunning, as the narrow road winds along the cliffs south of Carmel and Carmel Highlands. When there are whales in the area, they are frequently visible from one of the many roadside pullouts in Big Sur.

The panorama also features the Santa Lucia Mountains, sloping hillsides with the greenest grasses and shrubs, meadows with cows grazing next to the surf, redwood forests with dark green ferns covering the ground below, river canyons that cut in and out to the ocean and offshore rocks that are continually licked by white caps.

Big Sur ranges from foggy, when layers of clouds can hang along the rocky coastline like pillows, to sunshiny and cozy. It's a varied climate that is in wonderful harmony with the varied scenery.

A 15-mile drive can take you through such diversity that it can seem like a vacation in a single day.

There are some delightful restaurants here, hiking trails in the state and national parks, secluded beaches where clothing can be optional and famous hot tubs at places like the Esalen Institute.

Several Hollywood and recording celebrities live in the natural, "laid back" elegance here, as do some unknown recluses and holdout hippies.

There are said to be valuable marijuana gardens in the area, so it could be dangerous to wander off the main roads and trails.

Big Sur is deceptively easy to get to. Head south from Carmel and in about 15 minutes, you're there. On the way, you've crossed the Carmel River, passed the Carmelite Monastery, Point Lobos State Reserve and Carmel Highlands. Watch for the graceful Bixby Bridge, which has been used in hundreds of automobile commercials.

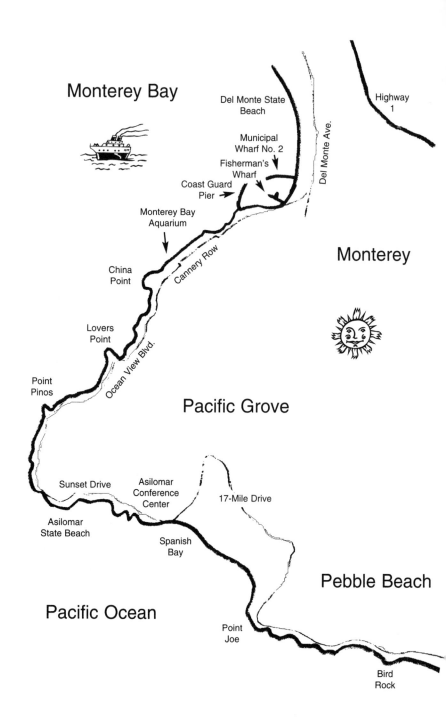

Monterey Bay

Del Monte State Beach

Municipal Wharf No. 2

Fisherman's Wharf

Coast Guard Pier

Monterey Bay Aquarium

China Point

Cannery Row

Del Monte Ave.

Highway 1

Monterey

Lovers Point

Ocean View Blvd.

Point Pinos

Pacific Grove

Sunset Drive

Asilomar Conference Center

17-Mile Drive

Asilomar State Beach

Spanish Bay

Pebble Beach

Pacific Ocean

Point Joe

Bird Rock

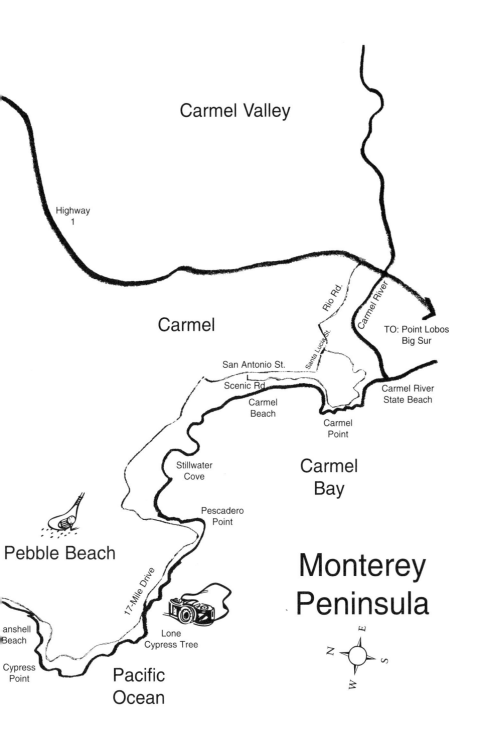

Carmel Valley

Highway
1

Carmel

Rio Rd.

Carmel River

TO: Point Lobos
Big Sur

San Antonio St.

Santa Lucia St.

Scenic Rd.

Carmel
Beach

Carmel River
State Beach

Carmel
Point

Stillwater
Cove

Carmel
Bay

Pescadero
Point

Pebble Beach

Monterey
Peninsula

17-Mile Drive

anshell
Beach

Lone
Cypress Tree

N E S W

Cypress
Point

Pacific
Ocean

Events and
Special Attractions

This place is like San Francisco in that it's almost impossible to spend a day without having a delightful time.

There's the ocean and that gorgeous shoreline, of course, the Santa Lucia Mountains and the forests, the views and the walks, the exercise for both body and spirit.

You can find your own pace and your own amusement here, as millions of people do each year.

Or you can follow my recommendations in the "SPECIAL TOURS" section of this book.

But however you do it, there are a few things you don't want to overlook while you're in the Monterey Peninsula-Carmel area. Here's a list of them:

• The **Monterey Bay Aquarium** at 886 Cannery Row in Monterey has to head any list of must-sees in the area. It is generally acclaimed as one of the finest, if not *the* finest aquarium in the nation.

The aquarium essentially brings the Monterey Bay indoors so you can see it. There are more than 500 species of fish living in the aquarium exhibits, which are filled with actual sea water piped in from the bay. I spend most of my time there adoring the playful sea otters, being mesmerized by the magical jellyfish or watching the video being broadcast live from the canyon on the floor of the bay, which drops about 10,000 feet deep and runs about 100 miles off shore.

The aquarium is open from 10 a.m. to 6 p.m. and charges $15.95 for adults, $6.95 for children under 12. It can be crowded at peak tourist seasons, with as many as 10,000 people in the aquarium per day. There's also a good little restaurant inside and a classy gift shop.

• **Carmel Mission Basilica** at 3080 Rio Road in Carmel, about a half-mile west of Highway 1, is the most interesting piece of architecture in the area.

It is one of the missions that Father Junipero Serra built when he led the Spanish to California in the 18th century. Serra, a candidate for Catholic sainthood despite native American protests that he enslaved their ancestors, is buried in the mission floor.

The graceful mission, which has been restored to its 1771 appearance, is, indeed, a treasured shrine. But it is also a functioning church with an elementary school attached. You can visit it as a museum as more than 250,000 people do each year, or attend one of the frequent Masses. There are no charges at the mission, but donations are always welcome.

•If you have time for only one stop to see nature at its finest, make it **Point Lobos State Reserve** off Highway 1, about four miles south of Carmel. The nature preserve has only one road for vehicles, but lots of trails for walking. There are trails along coves, onto headlands, through a forest of windswept cypress trees and through meadows of native grasses. Watch for sea otters in the water, sea lions on the offshore rocks, cormorants, pelicans and occasional whales passing by. In the spring, usually from about the middle of March to the end of April, watch for all the poppies and other wildflowers that seem to pop up everywhere.

Point Lobos may be the best, most compact glossary of all the natural beauty you can see along the Central California Coast. It is the place Robert Louis Stevenson used as the setting for "Treasure Island." Admission, from 7 a.m. to sunset, is $7.

•If you have time for only one scenic drive in the Monterey Peninsula-Carmel area, make it the **17-Mile Drive** through Pebble Beach. It's really a bargain at $7.50. (See details in the "SPECIAL TOURS" section of this book.)

There are five gates into the private community that all link up to 17-Mile Drive. There's one off Highway 1, immediately south of the Highway 68 route into Pacific Grove. There's another off Highway 68 at the Pacific Grove city limit, two in Pacific Grove — one off Congress Avenue, one off Sunset Drive — and one from Carmel, off North San Antonio Avenue.

If you want to save money, you can drive the five-mile coastline of Pacific Grove — Sunset Drive and Ocean View Boulevard — for free. It has the same stunning shoreline scenery, but not as many trees and almost no mansions.

You can also drive the two miles of Carmel's Scenic Road and see the city's snow-white beach, then lots of villa-like houses overlooking Carmel Bay.

•If you have time for a side trip, or if you're driving north on Highway 1 anyway, I'd recommend a stop at Moss Landing, at the **Elkhorn Slough National Estuarine Research Sanctuary** at 1700 Elkhorn Road.

It is another nature preserve, this one of wetlands. The slough snakes through the area, rising and falling with the ocean's tide, creating mudflats that are vital to the reproduction of nearly 500 species of animals.

The area is also a sanctuary for birds, attracting more than 100 species of shorebirds and migratory species who stop to feed in the slough.

• If you're going inland to Salinas, about 15 miles through beautiful hills, I'd recommend a stop at the **Steinbeck National Center** at 1 Main St. It's the only museum in the country devoted to a writer and it's amazing how interesting words can be presented. The Steinbeck Center uses movie clips, dioramas, posters, antiques and old pictures to make John Steinbeck's Nobel Prize-winning novels come alive near the places where they were written. It's open from 10 a.m. to 5 p.m. daily and charges $7 for adults, $4 for children over 10.

There are, as you might imagine, a lot of annual shows, festivals and events in the Monterey Peninsula-Carmel area that are worth attending. For exact dates each year, write or call the Monterey Peninsula Visitors & Convention Bureau at 380 Alvarado St., Monterey 93940, (831) 649-1770. Here are some to watch for:

• First or second week of January — The gray whale migration, with more than 20,000 of the gigantic animals swimming between Alaska and Mexico, usually peaks about this time.

• Late January or early February — The AT&T National Pro-Am Golf Tournament at Pebble Beach attracts top golf professionals, show-business and sports celebrities for a four-day event.

• April — The Big Sur International Marathon, an increasingly popular race along the beautiful coastline.

• Last weekend of May — The Great Monterey Squid Festival at the Monterey Fairgrounds, an event that features calamari cooked in every way imaginable.

• Last weekend of June — The Monterey Bay Blues Festival at the Monterey Fairgrounds brings in some of the biggest names in blues.

• Middle July to middle August — Carmel Bach Festival in Carmel.

• Late July — Feast of Lanterns celebration in Pacific Grove, an event that culminates in a charming Saturday night pageant at Lovers Point.

• August — Concours D'Elegance, a Pebble Beach show and auction of collectors' classic cars; and Historic Automobile Races at Laguna Seca Raceway, the running of vintage race cars.

• September — Indy Car World Series races at Laguna Seca Raceway.

• Middle September — Monterey Jazz Festival at the Monterey Fairgrounds, the grandfather of all of them.

• Middle December — Christmas in the Adobes in Monterey, where two dozen of the state-owned adobe buildings are decorated and opened for candlelight tours.

The Best Places for Walks

Walking is a major pastime here, for residents and tourists alike.

And why not? The Mediterranean climate usually lets you go outdoors in relative comfort and there is no shortage of beautiful, interesting places to walk.

You can generally feel pretty safe to wander down any street, any lane or any path here and look at the scenery or the houses. Use common sense and courtesy for the exceptions, and be leery of straying from the popular trails in Big Sur, where there are said to be marijuana growers who might be hostile to strangers.

But if you want suggestions for where to walk, here are some of the best places:

Beaches are popular, of course, and the best ones for walking are:

•**Del Monte State Beach**, which starts at Municipal Wharf No. 2 in Monterey and stretches along Monterey Bay several miles north before sand cliffs cut if off.

•**Asilomar State Beach**, which is the southern part of the Pacific Grove shoreline. The ocean beach is only a half-mile long, but it's attached to a two-mile coastal trail on the north, a boardwalk to Spanish Bay on the south.

•**Carmel Beach**, a mile-long crescent that can be found at the foot of Ocean Avenue. This is a beach that welcomes dogs, and there are usually lots of them.

•**Carmel River State Beach**, which stretches about two miles along Carmel Bay from the southern tip of Carmel to Monastery Beach alongside Highway 1. It's probably the purest, least-used beach in the area.

There are also a lot of walking and bicycling trails in the Monterey Peninsula-Carmel area. Here are the best:

•**The Monterey Bay Recreation Trail** runs four miles along the Monterey shoreline and to Lovers Point in Pacific Grove. It is the best, taking you along a stunning coast, through Cannery Row, around the Monterey harbor, past Del Monte State Beach and under a grove of aromatic eucalyptus trees. The most-popular section is the 2 1/2 miles from Fisherman's Wharf to Lovers Point.

•The two-mile-long **coastal trail** between Asilomar and Point Pinos in Pacific Grove. There's another trail north of Point Pinos, for the two miles to Lovers Point, but it's less paved.

•**Pebble Beach** has a trail along part of its coastline, with parts of it utilizing the shoulder of 17-Mile Drive, some of it on boardwalks and some through groves of the Del Monte Forest.

•**Point Lobos State Reserve** south of Carmel has wonderful trails everywhere. One of the best is a mile-long trail on a terrifically-scraggly coastline that the park calls the South Shore Trail. There's a more inland trail, the North Shore Trail, that stretches 1.4 miles through fields of wildflowers and forests of cypress and pine trees. And there's my favorite at the very southern tip of Point Lobos, the South Plateau Trail to China Cove, where I've seen more sea otters and their pups than anywhere else in the area.

•**Jacks Peak**, a county park at the highest point on the Monterey Peninsula, about 1,000 feet above sea level, has trails through pine and oak forests that open into panoramas of Monterey Bay and environs on the one side, Carmel Bay and environs on the other. (Jacks Peak is generally south of the Monterey Peninsula Airport. To get there, take Highway 68, the Salinas-Monterey Highway, to Olmsted Road and follow the signs.)

Remember where you are. In a place like this, walks through town can be enchanting. Here are some of the best:

•In Monterey, roam along **Alvarado Street** downtown to see how the town lives now, around the old buildings near **Fisherman's Wharf** to see how it used to live and through the **Presidio**, just for the delightful views of Monterey Bay.

•In **Pacific Grove**, walk through the old-fashioned downtown section and see how people lived before there were suburbs. Turn down any street and look at the frills on the **Victorian houses** the city is so proud of.

•In **Carmel**, the downtown area is famous as a shopping resort, but its European styling is worth close looks too. The residential streets are loaded with eye-catching houses and landscapes.

Rent-by-the-hour Adventures

People come here from all over the world to see the scenery, walk in the crisp sea air, eat in some distinguished restaurants, play golf and visit the Monterey Bay Aquarium.

While those may be the most popular things to do here, there are lots of other possibilities for fun and adventure. Here are some of them:

Take up **scuba diving**. There are hundreds of scuba divers entering the water off Monterey, Pacific Grove and Carmel almost every day. If you want to be one of them, call the Monterey scuba centers to check on prices, lessons, equipment rentals and facilities.
- Aquarius Dive Shop, 375-6605 or 375-1933.
- Bamboo Reef Enterprises, 372-1685.
- Monterey Bay Dive Center, 656-0454.

If you don't want to go under the water, try **ocean kayaking**. There are at least two outfits in Monterey that rent kayaks and offer lessons and tours. Kayaks rent for about $25 a day. You can arrange for them through:
- Adventures by the Sea, 372-1807.
- Monterey Bay Kayaks, 373-5357 (373-KELP).

For **ocean fishing**, there are four old-line companies on Fisherman's Wharf that operate what they call "party boats" for sport fishing. You pay about $30 to $125, depending on the day and the season, and leave from the wharf around 6 a.m. They will also rent you all the equipment you'll need for the day. The companies are:
- Monterey Sport Fishing, 372-2203.
- Randy's Fishing Trips, 372-7440.
- Chris' Fishing Trips, 375-5951.
- Sam's Fishing Fleet, 372-0577.

The fishing fleet offers **whale watching** in season, which is roughly Thanksgiving to Valentine's Day. More than 20,000 gray whales swim through Monterey Bay each year as they migrate between their summer feeding waters in the Gulf of Alaska and their winter breeding waters in Mexico. The migration usually peaks about the second week in January, with so many whales you think you can step from the back of one to another. The "party boats" charge about $15 for a memorable trip to the whales. It's a good way to get a bay cruise.

If you want to stay on land, you can rent **bicycles** at a number of places in Monterey and Carmel. Figure $6 to $10 for an hour, about $25 for the day. Check terms with:

- Adventures by the Sea in Monterey and Pacific Grove, 372-1807.
- Bay Bikes, 646-9090, and in Carmel, 625-2453 (625-BIKE).
- Freewheeling Cycles in Monterey, 373-3855.
- Monterey Moped Adventures, 373-2696.

If you want a motor on your bike, **mopeds** can be rented from Monterey Moped Adventures, 373-2696, from $20 for the first hour to $50 for the day.

For wheels on your own feet, you can rent in-line **skates** from Adventures by the Sea, 372-1807, at either the Monterey or the Pacific Grove end of the paved Monterey Bay Recreation Trail. They're $12 for two hours to $24 for a day.

For a pure **workout**, the Monterey Sports Center across from Fisherman's Wharf offers a weight room, swimming pool and indoor basketball courts for $5.50 for adults, $3.50 for young folks. Call 646-3730 for hours and specifics.

Public **tennis** courts with lights for night play sit near the sports center. The Monterey Tennis Center charges $3 an hour per person for a court and an extra $1 for the lights. It's open seven days and five nights a week. Call 646-3881 to reserve a court.

There are 125 tennis facilities in the Monterey Peninsula-Carmel area, but this is the only public one that lights up at night.

The **paddlewheel boats** in Lake El Estero, across Del Monte Avenue from the wharf, rent for $7 per half-hour.

And if you insist there's nothing better to do here than to **play golf**, there are 20 courses to choose from, with greens fees ranging from $320 at the world-renowned Pebble Beach Golf Links to $35 at the city-owned course in Pacific Grove. You can play with Clint Eastwood here, but memberships in his private golf club, Tehema, start at $100,000.

Best Places
to Take Pictures

This place seems to be a photographer's dream. Trust your eyes, the amazing beauty is real.

But I'm usually disappointed with my pictures here. The ocean turns out to be not as blue as I remembered. The sunset is just a burst of white light. The sea otter that was so cute is just a distant blur in the photo. And the enlargement from my 35-mm negative is so fuzzy and out of focus it's not worth framing.

Somehow my pictures aren't as good as the ones on post cards and calendars. So I've learned to keep them simpler than my awe.

For example, instead of a sweeping beach scene, I have better luck photographing my dog as he splashes through the surf just off shore. There's enough ocean in the background and sand in the foreground that you can see the scene while looking at an interesting picture.

But if you want a good shoreline shot, as most of us do, let me suggest you try these:

• The famous **Carmel Beach**, a mile-long crescent of snow-white sand that starts at the foot of Ocean Avenue, the main street in town, and runs alongside Scenic Road, which has parking spaces and wooden stairways down to the beach. I would shoot it from either end, at street level, so I could catch the crescent-shaped shoreline wrapping around the ocean. I would also frame the scene through the statuesque cypress trees that can be found near either end of the beach.

• The **Lone Cypress tree**, which sits on a rock off 17-Mile Drive in Pebble Beach, between Cypress Point and Pescadero Point. The tree, which is the official symbol of Monterey County, sits far enough off shore that it can be photographed on top of its colorful rock with ocean surf in the foreground. On a clear day, Point Lobos, which is a few miles across Carmel Bay, forms a good background that helps define the coastal scene and give it a perspective.

• **Cypress Point** offers some possibilities when the sun is right. There are cypress trees on the north and a cove on the south, either of which can frame a surging-surf shot.

In the late winter and early spring months, the parking lot at Cypress Point is closed to vehicles and the shoreline is blocked by a plywood wall.

That's because the harbor seals are having and nursing their pups on the beaches there, a wondrous event that makes the mothers so nervous they will abandon their pups to instant death if they are disturbed. But there are peep holes in the wall, so if you're quiet and have a long lens for your camera, you can photograph one of the most touching scenes on the Monterey Peninsula.

•**Lovers Point** in Pacific Grove is a nice divider for two totally different picture possibilities. The ice plant on the shoreline south of the point flowers into a beautiful pink carpet in the springtime, a scene that makes a nice picture on its own or serves as a pretty foreground for a broader coastal shot. North of Lovers Point, for a mile up to Cannery Row, is a rocky shoreline that I believe is the most beautiful stretch on the Monterey Peninsula. It has a series of small, sandy coves between rocky outcroppings so scenic photos can be taken almost anywhere along there.

•The best sunsets are shot from the Pacific Grove shoreline, anywhere on the two-mile stretch from **Asilomar State Beach** on the city's southern border to **Point Pinos**, where the bay breaks away from the open ocean. There are lots of rocks and sandy strips in there to form foregrounds for the ocean waves and the sun that sets due west.

•**Point Lobos State Reserve** just south of Carmel, marking the southern tip of Carmel Bay, offers one of the most beautiful and varied shorelines in the area. There's an easy walking trail all alongside it. For better pictures, walk out on the points and shoot back towards the coves along the rocky shoreline instead of shooting the other way, out at the open ocean, where there's no frame for perspective.

•The **Big Sur coast** along Highway 1 south of Carmel offers an endless panorama. You can stop about anywhere and find a picture worth framing. My favorite is from the parking area south of the Bixby Bridge, looking back at the graceful arch you've seen in 100 car commercials. That's approximately 10 miles south of Carmel.

About five miles later, there's a giant rock off shore that has the Point Sur Lighthouse on top of it, an active surf around it.

And then I like the rocky outcroppings along Big Sur especially when they are covered and obscured by layers of fog. There are some beautiful, melancholy pictures there if you work it right.

The fog is something to keep in mind here. Summers frequently have heavy fogs in the mornings and evenings, usually with clear, warmer conditions in the middle of the day. The fog can interfere with your pictures, or it can provide tone, a soft frame, a feeling of mystery.

By the way, if you just want a picture of someone standing beside the ocean, you can take that almost anywhere along the shoreline here. If you want to be in the picture too, you can usually get a passerby to use your camera and shoot it for you. This is a fairly-relaxed resort, so most people are cooperative that way.

When you're finished with the shoreline, here are some other pictures that are fun to line up:

• The **boats** at Fisherman's Wharf.

• The old **adobe buildings** and houses in downtown Monterey, which go back more than 200 years to the Spanish period. (Tip: Try to get some of the native plants in the photos.)

• The **Victorian houses** in Pacific Grove, which go back more than a century to the Methodist founders. Just walk around the streets of the quiet little town until you find something you want to photograph. The people who live there are used to it.

• The **cute cottages** in Carmel, some of which go back to the turn of the century, when the resort was an artists' colony.

• The unusual critters, like the **sea otters**, an endangered species of cuddly little mammals that can usually be seen swimming and feeding in the Monterey marina and along Pacific Grove, or training their pups in the coves around Point Lobos. (Yes, they float on their backs, put shellfish on their stomachs and break them open with rocks so they can get to the meat.)

There are also **sea lions** parked on the rocks at the end of the Coast Guard Pier and just about everywhere else in the area.

Harbor seals can usually be found perched around Lovers Point. And **gray whales** can sometimes be found right along the shoreline, at the peak of their winter migration.

• The **covered bridge** over Cannery Row that links two buildings in the 700 block that were part of the sardine capital of the world in the 1920s, '30s and '40s.

• **Wildflowers**, if you happen to be here in late March or in April. They can be found virtually everywhere, but the prettiest fields may be at Point Lobos, Jacks Peak or along the Salinas-Monterey Highway.

Wines Worth Drinking

I've all but given up my search for a good $10 wine. Oh, you can still find one occasionally, but you have to drink a lot of swill along the way.

I find I'm paying closer to $15 for most of my chardonnay these days, sometimes up to $20, and about the same for the reds that I drink less often. It breaks my heart, but at least there are plenty of good wines to choose from in that price range. (These, by the way, are retail prices. Restaurants generally double them.)

I pretty much limit myself to Monterey County wines now because I try to stay current. There are so many local wines — 160 varieties from about 30 wineries the last time I tried to taste them all — that it's tough to keep up year in and year out. God knows I try.

Fortunately a lot of the local wines are good these days. Some are pretty bad, to be sure, and some are grossly overpriced.

I've gotten into trouble for saying that's there's both good and bad here. Some people want to pretend there's nothing less than perfect in Monterey County, but that's either dreamland or a marketing ploy.

I once did a list in descending order, starting with the wines I thought were the best and going down to the ones I thought were awful. I thought it was good news that I found more good than bad, something that couldn't have been said here a decade ago. But some winemakers yelled and screamed anyway, while others told me privately they generally agreed with my list.

I actually like about two-thirds of the local wines these days. Some of them are so overpriced I don't buy them, but I like to find them at the one-price-covers-all wine tastings that are becoming more frequent. In the meantime there are enough good wines in the more-reasonable price ranges that you don't have to buy the overpriced ones.

Chardonnay

Good chardonnays are the easiest to find here because the soils and climates of Monterey County are best for that variety. Fortunately I love chardonnay.

The Monterey County chardonnays — the good ones — are fruity and a bit to the dry side. (The bads ones are like grapefruit juice.)

The best for the past several years have come from **Bernardus Winery** in Carmel Valley, which has consistently produced a superb chardonnay since 1992. It's a little fuller than most of the local chardonnays, smoother with some of the butter you find in good Napa Valley chardonnays. It sells for about $18 a bottle.

Lockwood Vineyard in the Salinas Valley has also made consistently good chardonnays since the early 1990s. They sell in the $16 range.

Near Lockwood, **Scheid Vineyards** has also made good chardonnays in recent years in the $16 range.

For more money, generally $27 retail, **Chalone Vineyard** has some chardonnays that are hard to beat. They tend to be drier than the lowland wines, but with grapey tastes that awaken your mouth.

For value, I look for **Hahn Estates**, which produced excellent 1996 and 1997 chardonnays for $10 a bottle; **Ventana Vineyards'** "Gold Stripe" chardonnay for $12; or **Cloninger Cellars**, which produced an excellent 1997 chardonnay for $10 a bottle.

I also watch for the **J. Lohr Winery**, which has produced some excellent chardonnays from its Riverstone Vineyards for about $13; **Morgan Winery**, which has had some good years and some bad in the $20 range; and **Joullian Vineyards**, which had a terrific 1996 for about $15.

For snob appeal, let's have a word about the **Robert Talbott Vineyard**. It makes a drier, French-style chardonnay for about $35 a bottle. It is good wine, but for the money I would much rather have two bottles of Bernardus, or three of Hahn.

Other white wines

Other whites tend to do well in Monterey County conditions, too, but they aren't as popular as the chardonnays. If you're looking for a sauvignon blanc, I think Bernardus and Joullian bottle the best. For reislings, try **Paraiso Springs Vineyard** or **Jekel Vineyards**.

If you want one of the newer, dry whites, Paraiso Springs 1996 pinot blanc at about $13 is the best, Chalone's at $26 is terrific and Lockwood's at $16 is good.

Cabernet sauvignon

Local red wines tend to be pretty bold, but there are some good ones. I'm partial to cabernet sauvignon and like the older ones better than the young ones, as they've had time to smooth out.

I truly love the **Smith & Hook Winery's** cabs from 1994 and 1995, which retail for about $18 a bottle. A sister winery, Hahn, puts out lighter cabs for about $10 a bottle and its 1996 vintage is easily worth twice that.

The Lockwood cabernet from 1994, Scheid from 1995, Cloninger from the middle '90s and Joullian from the early '90s are also good, Bordeaux-style wines.

Other reds

There are some good merlots here, too, notably the Ventana 1993, the Lockwood 1993 and the Hahn 1994.

For different reds, Ventana makes a very decent Syrah, and Lockwood has an impressive chianti-style Sangiovese, both for about $16.

Pinot noir has proven tricky here, though lots of wineries are trying it because it's so marketable these days. There are some very bad ones, but I have found a few that I could recommend. From the 1996 vintage, try Chalone for $26, Paraiso Springs for $23 or Morgan for $19.

Tours and tastes

If you've got the time, it's really kind of fun to visit the wineries and sample for yourself. There aren't many fullblown tours of the vineyards, crushing operations, barrel rooms and bottling lines here like there are in Napa Valley. But several of the wineries now have public tasting rooms where you can sample the products.

You probably should call ahead to check on the tasting room and see when it's open, since most of the wineries here are small and don't have enough staff to open them daily.

And you should definitely keep the designated-driver rule in mind, since most of the local wineries are on rural roads where traffic and turns can be tricky.

The wineries generally line up along three different paths:

•Carmel Valley Road, straight east of Highway 1 along the Carmel River, where Bernardus Winery, Durney Vineyards and Chateau Julien Wine Estate have public tasting rooms. Four other Carmel Valley wineries have tastings on occasions and take part in special events.

•River Road, which runs south from Monterey-Salinas Highway 68 along the Salinas River, where Cloninger Cellars, Smith & Hook Winery, Hahn Estates and Paraiso Springs Vineyards have public tasting rooms.

•Highway 101 in the Salinas Valley south of Salinas, where Jekel Vineyards and Scheid Vineyards have tasting rooms. Chalone Vineyard is open too, in the beautiful hills east of Soledad.

About the Bars and Nightlife Here

Nobody comes to the Monterey Peninsula-Carmel area for the nightlife, so don't get your hopes up that it will be exciting.

This is an early-to-bed, early-to-rise type of place because most people come here for the scenery and nature and things most visible and enjoyable in daylight.

Evening entertainment usually centers around dinner and, on good nights, romance.

There are movies, plays and concerts, of course, listed in the daily paper. And there are bars. But I need to caution you about them.

•**Carmel** doesn't allow music in its bars, so don't go looking for a show there or a place to dance. Its bars are strictly for drinking, usually in conjunction with restaurants. Some of them are pretty good, but can be noisy.

•**Pacific Grove** doesn't have any bars to speak of. It was the last city in California to allow liquor sales and, then, only so its restaurants could compete with other resort eateries.

•**Pebble Beach** has bars only as attachments to its restaurants, hotels and golf courses. They can be difficult to find if you're not already there.

•**Big Sur** has a narrow, winding road along steep cliffs to keep in mind, unless you're staying where you are drinking.

•**Monterey** has a lot of bars, but some of them are neighborhood-kind of places that aren't particularly inviting, with rows of motorcycles out front and that sort of thing. Others have music, bands and dance floors.

MONTEREY

Downtown, near the big hotels, is pretty iffy for nightlife. There are usually a lot of people on the streets and a sense that something's happening. But if you're at least 22 years old you might feel uncomfortable at many of the places around Alvarado Street.

There are a few exceptions, but I'm reluctant to cite many because the bars downtown tend to be trendy. British-type pubs seem to be this year's fad, in places filled with pool tables last year, rock bands the year before, big-screen sports before that and disc jockeys, live comedy, disco, folk music or whatever other trend looked profitable.

Feel free to stroll around and see for yourself. The area is one of the safest in the country, heavily policed and watched by people who have huge investments in their businesses there.

Let me just mention two places downtown in particular.

Cibo, sort of across from the Doubletree and Marriott at the corner of Alvarado Street and Del Monte Avenue, has music on weekend nights. It may be jazz, rock, reggae or salsa, but the place is usually crowded with adults who like to dance.

LALLApalooza Restaurant further down the street at 474 Alvarado St. is one of the latest hot spots, a martini bar with food that can be busy and noisy.

If you venture to Cannery Row at night, you can find some other places that are usually pretty lively. Here are two:

Doc's Nightclub in a basement at the corner of Prescott and Wave streets, a block up from Cannery Row, usually has rock bands that crank up late at night.

Planet Gemini upstairs at 625 Cannery Row also has rock music usually, sometimes country or comedy, in its large nightclub.

For a quieter time, the Hyatt Regency frequently has a jazz trio on the weekends. Or you might try the bar at the **Stokes Adobe Restaurant**, where you can hear each other talk.

CARMEL

Carmel-by-the-Sea, one of the best known resorts in the world, has most of its bars in conjunction with restaurants. Most of them are small holding areas where people can sip while waiting for tables.

One notable exception is the bar at **La Playa Hotel** at 8th Avenue and Camino Real. It is one of the classiest bars in town, large and woody and comfortable. And it's one of the quieter places, so you can just kick back and talk. Or drink.

A few others worth noting are the bars at:

General Store-Forge in the Forest at the corner of 5th Street and Junipero Avenue, where you want to sit outdoors by the fireplaces at night.

Britannia Arms in Su Vencino Court, between Dolores and Lincoln Streets just north of 6th Avenue, which has a British feeling and a selection of beers on tap.

Jack London's Restaurant on San Carlos Street near 5th Avenue, which is frequented by residents and serves food late.

Just outside of the city limits, there's the speakeasy-style bar at the **Mission Ranch**, a place usually crowded by older people at night who sing along with the piano player, and the lively bar at the **Rio Grill**. Both sometimes have celebrities in their midsts.

Shopping

Lots of people come to this area just to shop, which sort of amazes me. I always think of the natural beauty here and the crisp, sea air, not the funk or the fashions.

But I have lived here long enough to know where the shopping areas are, and how each differs from the others.

Here's my guide:

•**Del Monte Shopping Center** in Monterey, on Munras Avenue just off Highway 1, is the largest and most traditional shopping center in the area. It has more than 100 stores, shops and restaurants, with Macy's and Mervyn's as the anchors.

•**The Crossroads Shopping Center** at the mouth of Carmel Valley, on Rio Road just off Highway 1, is yuppier with no large stores other than a Longs Drug Store and a Safeway. It has several good restaurants among the 60 or so stores in the center.

•**The Barnyard Shopping Center** is across Rio Road from The Crossroads, alongside Highway 1. It's got some pretty fancy clothing stores among its 40 or so tenants. The center seems to be anchored by the Thunderbird.

•**Carmel** attracts bus loads of people who want to shop in the downtown area. Many pour into **Carmel Plaza** on Ocean Avenue and Junipero Street, which has about 50 shops in a three-story building designed around an interior plaza. And many roam through the commercial district, which has lots of gift stores, specialty shops, antiques and more than 70 art galleries sprinkled throughout the streets, courtyards and plazas of the European-like village.

•The discount stores are in Pacific Grove, in a large outlet center called **American Tin Cannery**. It's on Ocean View Boulevard near the city's boundary with Monterey, just a block from Cannery Row and the Monterey Bay Aquarium. It has about 50 stores, most of them clothing and gift stores set up in serve-yourself, warehouse style.

Moving to Monterey

A Newcomer's Guide
to the Peninsula Paradise

By Thom Akeman

Taken from his "First Impressions" columns
in *The Monterey Peninsula Herald*

Illustrated by Irene Lagorio

About the Reprint That Follows

When I first moved to the Monterey Peninsula, I wrote a weekly column in the paper that is now The Monterey County Herald. It chronicled the findings and experiences of a newcomer on the Monterey Peninsula.

The columns described parks, trails, scenic drives, sunsets, moonlight on the bay, the beauty of ocean storms, dolphins flickering through the waves, whales, sea otters entertaining along the shoreline, herds of deer grazing on golf courses, the high cost of living, the problems finding reasonable housing and the thrills of brushing elbows with the show business celebrities who live here.

There were also columns about local restaurants, local wines, bars and festivals.

We were surprised by the popularity of the newcomer columns. They got a lot of attention, and a lot of mail.

After a year, we rounded up the columns and reprinted them as a paperback book titled "Moving to Monterey, a Newcomer's Guide to the Peninsula Paradise."

The first printing in 1988 sold out, as did a second. The book vanished from bookstore shelves in 1992 and has been turning up in garage sales ever since.

But people kept asking for it, the bookstore folks tell me.

So ego has driven me to reprint the book in this slightly varied form.

Most of the original columns are reprinted as they appeared in the paper, then in the book. Some of the stuff in them is dated, like the prices of things. But keeping the original form and sequence preserves the flavor and the pacing of a newcomer's discoveries. It was also cheaper to use the old type.

I've tried to update the columns with new information at the front of this book — up-to-date restaurant reviews, lists of the neat things I've found here and current essays about the distinguishable communities in this peninsula resort.

Without the updates, you've got a set of popular columns. With them, you've got a guidebook.

—*Thom Akeman*

The Peninsula —
Only the Beginning

It's a pretty T-shirt, ocean-blue with orange letters on it.

A gift from a guy I used to work with, it says simply: "I died and went to Monterey."

It's nice, in a lot of ways.

And it ignited a brief conversation last month when I wore it at a motel swimming pool while visiting relatives in heat-buckled Illinois.

A woman from Missouri, splashing around the pool with a couple of tiny kids, spotted the shirt and said, "Ooooh, that's a beautiful place, and right at the foot of the Golden Gate Bridge."

Well, I agreed with her that Monterey is a beautiful place. And I decided not to argue about its proximity to the Golden Gate Bridge — partly because I didn't see the point of arguing California geography with a woman who splashes around motel swimming pools in the Midwest, partly because I really wasn't so sure.

No, no, it wasn't the steamy heat of my birthplace taking control. And I'm not really that dumb.

But I'm not so sure right now just exactly what I do and don't know about Monterey.

Of course I know it's not at the foot of the Golden Gate Bridge. Some lesser cities are.

But I'm really not sure whether there's some other spectacular bridge here that I don't know about, some bridge dramatic enough to be mistaken for the one in San Francisco by a tourist or some other brief visitor.

You may know. And you may be saying right now that I must be a jerk without eyes in my head.

On the other hand, you may be reciting the name of the Golden Gate-like bridge and thinking about sending me a note to direct me to the heretofore-unobserved structure. If that's the case, let me thank you in advance.

For on my own, I don't know one way or the other about bridges. Yet.

That's just one of the things I expect to learn in the next few months while I explore Monterey and settle into the Peninsula as one of its newest residents. I'll tell you about it as I learn it.

I just moved here, see, to take a new job as a reporter for this newspaper, *The Herald.* This is, in fact, my very first week in town.

And though I've visited the area a dozen times over the years, I've always been a tourist, looking for something in particular. I now know Monterey as little more than a picture post card. I know some of the gorgeous bay views, for example. And I know about the monkey at the old wharf and the proximity to Big Sur.

But I've just started to realize how little that really is, how little I really know about the Monterey Peninsula.

It will take some time to learn about the bridges. And about the people and the way they live, about the tourists and the way they play, about the landlords, the groceries, the gas stations and movie houses, the tennis courts and bars, the traffic patterns, seasons, gulls, the fishing boats and all the other things that give Monterey breath.

I really know much less than I wonder. A dozen trips — including a sort-of honeymoon or two and some family vacations — really doesn't tell you all that much about a chosen home.

So while I was taking a long and strangely directed route to get here, the woman in the motel swimming pool made me wonder just what anybody else in the distance might know about Monterey. I wondered just how this place is perceived, before I get bogged down in close-ups and facts.

I asked the relatives and friends in Illinois — (yes, I know it seems bizarre to vacation in a climatic wasteland when you're enroute to paradise. I'll spare you the family history if you'll give me some rope on this one) — what they knew about Monterey. Most of them placed it in California all right. The veterans recalled Fort Ord.

But in fairness, I know most of those folks to be sweltering, land-locked people who don't get around all that much.

So I asked others who are a little closer to the coast — in Sacramento, where I have worked the past 10 years as a reporter for the *Sacramento Bee.*

Now mind you, most of the people I know in Sacramento are bright folks who are prone to hard work and heavy drink. Some of them are on the state payroll, of course, but many of them are newspaper reporters and editors who have no known felony convictions and are allowed to travel freely.

I asked a bunch of them about Monterey and there was no end to the information, suggestions and recommendations that came pouring from their mouths.

Why, nearly everyone mentioned the aquarium, the 17-Mile Drive, Lovers Point in Pacific Grove and the fishing wharf in Monterey. There were a couple of votes for the beach at Point Lobos, the shops in Carmel and the races at Laguna Seca. Some people mentioned bicycling along the ocean. One told about playing golf in pouring rain at Pebble Beach because the greens fee was so high and had to be paid in advance.

The fog got mentioned endlessly and housing costs came up a lot.

Enough Sacramentans travel to Monterey regularly that many of my friends recommended a favorite restaurant or two here. In all, five names came up. But the one most recommended by the people I know in Sacramento is an obscure little place I already knew about — the Sandbar and Grill under Wharf No. 2.

I was surprised at how many people know about this smaller wharf down at the marina. It's always been one of my favorite parts of Monterey.

Above the Sandbar, there's a little diner called Joe's Bait Shop, or something like that, where I invariably ate breakfast when I visited. The food wasn't so good, but Joe's always had some real fishermen hanging around in the morning, talking about fishing and tides and things of the sea.

I like to listen to that kind of talk. It always seemed so truly Monterey to me.

Now that perception may change after I've lived here for a while, of course. And maybe some day I'll even feel like arguing about Monterey with somebody in a Midwestern swimming pool.

But first, I have a lot of people to meet.

A surprising number of my friends in Sacramento claimed to have good friends living on the Peninsula. Why, just at the office going-away party I picked up the names of a restaurant owner, a hotel manager, a musician, a professional golfer, a doctor, a shoemaker and a school-teacher.

I was also told to say "Hi" to Mayor Clint about a hundred times . . . maybe two hundred.

Seeks Apartment,
Gets an Education

If you're going to settle into Monterey, first you have to find a place to live.

That may seem to be an easy thing to do and maybe even fun. There was a time I thought so, too.

That was a couple of weeks ago, when I started to look for an apartment to rent. I planned to become one of the newest residents of the Peninsula so I could work as a reporter for *The Herald*.

And I really thought.... Well, just let me tell you about my apartment-hunting experience, okay?

Now you have to understand that I had decided to rent because I was selling a house in Sacramento and didn't want to get bogged down in so many real estate details it would be a relief to settle here, instead of a pleasure.

And I decided it should be an apartment because I really don't need to do any more yard work in this lifetime.

I also decided it should have two bedrooms, even though I'm single and usually live alone. I wanted the second bedroom as an office. I also expect a lot of out-of-town company, now that I live in a place people want to visit.

So that was it. A two-bedroom apartment somewhere on the Peninsula. Close to the ocean, of course. And that's all I had in mind when I set off from Sacramento on a Thursday morning, convinced I would have a divine-yet-functional apartment locked up by bedtime.

Now it may be important here to point out that I was a little hung over at the time. I'd had a long, leisurely dinner with a friend the night before, one of those memorably warm dinners that can keep residual alcohol puffing through your brain for the next several days. We justified it this time as a farewell dinner.

But the important point is that I arrived in Monterey a little beaten up on the day I was going to find my new apartment.

I thought I wanted to live in the city of Monterey, the section called New Monterey or Pacific Grove.

My thinking was pretty vague on that and based on little more than driving along the coastal routes during a dozen visits. I was pretty sure that people who work for wages couldn't afford to live in Carmel or Pebble Beach.

But to deal with the rent . . . You can be arbitrary at first, but you have to pick a price range so you can categorize the apartments from overpriced to outrageously expensive and avoid looking at every rental in the area. Especially if you have a hangover.

I decided to start looking at the $500-a-month level. And if you didn't just stop reading to chuckle, it means that you haven't looked at rents on the Peninsula for a while. Believe me, there's nothing available for $500 a month. Nothing. Nada. Zero. Zip.

Oh, wait, I may have to take that back. I believe there was a garage in Carmel that could be rented for $500 a month. But if I understood the terms, you could only sleep while sitting in a bucket seat and you couldn't stay in the place overnight.

If you wanted an actual apartment, you had to pay extra. A lot extra.

The very cheapest two-bedroom apartment advertised that Thursday was $550 a month. And there was only one of them.

The next cheapest apartment in Monterey, New Monterey or Pacific Grove that day was $575. Then $595. Then there were a half-dozen ranging up to $700 a month. But there were dozens of places in the next price range, between $700 and $800 a month. And there were dozens more above that.

Obviously, this was going to be more expensive that I had figured. But I decided to start by looking at the $550 apartment, holding out the same hopeless dream that makes me buy lottery tickets in supermarkets.

Actually, I've had better luck with the lottery.

Here's what I saw for $550 a month: A congested complex off David Avenue that consists of three-story, rectangular buildings that look like they were designed by Motel 6. The balcony of the vacant apartment offered views of other apartment houses and the dozens of kids below, playing on the dirt where grass might have been.

The cheapest apartment in town looked like it was part of a public housing project, the kind of place no one chooses to live. I assumed it was our military payroll at work.

For $575, you could have lived on David Avenue itself . . . in one of the pits sandwiched in between the several delightful parts of that spotty street.

The $595 place was in New Monterey and offered a stupendous view of the bay, four blocks away. But it also had a front door screen ripped open, beer cans all over the sidewalk, a chopped motorcycle in the driveway and yapping dogs across the street. The place just didn't seem restful.

Did I mention that it backed up to an all-night gas station?

Actually I looked at several apartments in New Monterey, that section generally between Fisherman's Wharf and aquarium parking. But I decided generally that the apartments are too small, the area too congested and the streets too filled with young people who might like to listen to loud music late at night.

There's a much more pleasant section of apartments on the other side of the wharf, in the numbered streets just east of Monterey's El Estero Park.

I was about to rent a decent apartment on Park Avenue for what I thought was a bargain price of $650 . . . just when a jet bound for Monterey Peninsula Airport thundered overhead and drowned out the landlord's presentation.

The price I was willing to pay was going up as the day went on.

Eventually, the day became two and by Friday afternoon I had looked at 30 apartments for rent — most of the listings in *The Herald*'s classified section. I drove more than 100 miles in that small area and got depressed by some of the crap that rents for so many dollars.

It's harder to rent an apartment here than it is to buy a house in most places. Which may be exactly why we all want to be here anyway.

But after two days of serious looking, I found one truly good apartment and two others that would do if they had to. That's one out of 10, if you're keeping score.

The good one had strings attached to it, of course.

It was in Pacific Grove, that wonderfully funky and posh place that Carmel is trying to model itself after. And it was in one of those old Victorians, just a few houses in from the ocean. It was a huge apartment for $715 a month. And I really wanted it.

It was unlike most of the apartments I had looked at — sterile and box-like places designed for the convenience of the developers, with motel feelings and nothing at all inviting you to unpack and settle in.

But there was a waiting list and interviews scheduled for Sunday so the out-of-town owner could decide who should live in her terrific rental.

I couldn't wait around until Sunday. So I called her on the phone several times, talked to her brother-in-law in Monterey and drove to San Jose to be interviewed that Friday afternoon.

I really turned on the old charm.

And if that didn't work out . . .

Well, it didn't.

The owner called Sunday to say she had found a nice young couple to rent to, not a single man who might have his reporter friends in and get rowdy.

So I didn't have a place to live after all. But I was moving to Monterey anyway. I was going to have to park a U-Haul truck at a motel and find something quickly.

I was fairly angry about it. But I had learned a whole lot about housing.

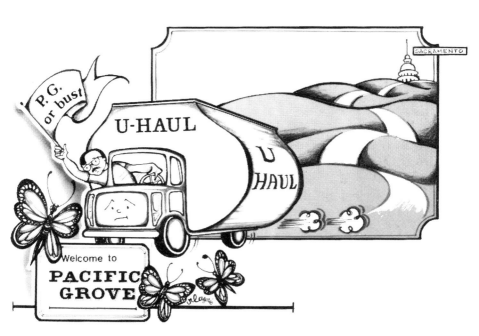

Captivated by a
Glimpse of the Bay

I swear I don't know where all the stuff comes from.

I threw out a lot of it, put a lot in storage, had a gigantic garage sale and still I packed for three days.

When I got finished I had boxes stacked all over the house. Scores of boxes.

And I really didn't know what was in any of them.

You know exactly what happened. I had to look for an unlisted number at the last minute and thought my phone book was in one of the boxes in that room. Or one of them in that one. Or . . .

What a pain!

But I really couldn't figure out what all the stuff was. Or why I had it. Or what I did with it. Or where I had kept it.

By the time I had it all packed, none of it had any value.

It was just so much bother in life.

I thought about torching it for the insurance and going off to live out of a sleeping bag. Ah, what freedom that must be.

I thought about asking the Salvation Army to come get it all so I wouldn't have to deal with it ever again.

I thought about just leaving it all behind and trying to argue that a new law required that I leave all that stuff in that house.

God knows, the idea of carrying all of those boxes and chairs and tables and mattresses to a U-Haul truck, driving it to a new place, carrying it into an apartment, unpacking it, sorting through it and arranging some of it, storing the rest, had absolutely no appeal on the third day of packing.

It didn't help that this was happening in Sacramento, in heat that pushed to 104 degrees Fahrenheit.

But even in decent weather the volume would have been overwhelming.

I think I got some insight into why some people just stay in houses they don't like. Or towns. Or jobs.

Moving is awful.

Especially when you're moving out of a house you've lived in for 10 years, with all the forgotten closets full and all the nooks and crannies and the garage loft you overlooked before the run to the dump.

You sort and pack and throw away and give away and sell and sort some more. Then you scramble to the liquor store dumpsters to get more boxes so you can sort and pack some more.

All the while, your emotions are getting nasty. Dismantling a nest takes hundreds of individual decisions, all of which have to be made while saying goodbye to friends and neighbors and colleagues who have to be left behind. Then there are the absolute strangers who are buying the house, standing around talking about tearing out the kitchen as if it weren't yours. And you're sort of worrying about your new job, which you're starting to resent because that's why you're going through all of this emotional upheaval anyway.

Put the physical labor of moving on top of that, then try to be patient with an electric company clerk who doubts you when you tell her you don't yet have a new address for the final bill. She just didn't believe it could be so hard to find a decent apartment in a place like Monterey.

Actually, the electric company on that end and the phone company on this one were the only external problems I had in moving to the Monterey Peninsula. Most institutions have made it easier since I last moved 10 years ago.

Even the phone company tried. A very pleasant woman in the Monterey office of Pacific Bell carefully explained all the options and costs in today's phone system: measured versus flat rates, no listing or multiples, referrals from your old number, rotary or touch-tone dialing, zone rates or long distance, choose a long distance company, call forwarding? Call waiting? Maintenance insurance for the lines inside your home?

And while she did her job, we talked about the weather and expenses here and in the Central Valley. And we laughed about comedienne Lily Tomlin's put-downs of the phone company.

And then true to form, we were disconnected before we finished our business.

The pay phone I was using broke down while I was talking to the phone company.

So I went to another phone booth, called again and was put on hold.

It should have been predictable.

The phone company is the only universal I've found in all the places I've ever lived. Other things sometimes work.

But I'm getting ahead of my story. Before I could get a phone here, I had to get an apartment.

Now you may remember that my two-day apartment-hunting trip was a general bust. It produced a lot of overpriced disappointments, but no rentable housing.

So when it was time to move, we loaded the truck in Sacramento, some friends and I, and drove it to Monterey.

The remorse set in on the four-hour drive down. My mind, which had become a marshmallow from the strain of so many decisions and so many farewells, decided that I had made a terrible mistake. I was giving up a secure job, a comfortable house and some irreplaceable friends to move to a resort area where I knew no one and didn't even have a place to live.

Just when I decided I had no choice but to turn around and go back and start unwinding the mess I had made for myself, I pulled over the sand dunes near Marina and got a fresh glimpse of this gorgeous bay and a blast of cool air. Well, hell, I thought, maybe I'll just wait a few years then think about going back.

It's really that easy to be captivated by this place. And everything was

OK after that.

My friends and I parked the loaded truck in the parking lot of one of my favorites — Borg's Motel in Pacific Grove. Then we opened a bottle of wine.

We looked through the latest apartment ads in *The Herald* and made a list of the ones we wanted to look at on the way to dinner.

Any one of them would have done at that point. But I finally got lucky. The best of the bunch was right around the corner, a half-block from Lovers Point.

It's in one of those funky old Victorians, just three houses from a bed-and-breakfast that gets $185 a night. Of course it has a full view of Monterey Bay through one large window, a panorama of city lights through another.

It's a better apartment than the one I didn't get a block away. It's closer to the water, newly remodeled inside and it has a fireplace that works. I moved in the next day so I could get started unpacking and sorting through all my stuff.

But still, I can't help thinking that I should walk over to the place that got away and tell the tenants that beat me out of it that I was offered their place for $300 less than they are paying. I think that might be fun.

Meeting the Neighbors and Settling In

I can just sit there in the window and watch the boats float by in the bay.

I can wave at the kayaks, count the scuba divers on any given weekend, look across and see the smoke stacks of Moss Landing and wonder where all the gulls are flying to. Or from.

Sometimes I can hear the sea otters barking. Sometimes I can hear the wind pushing through the cypress trees. Sometimes I can hear the waves rolling against the rocks of the coastline.

Always I can feel the fresh air coming in from the ocean.

And those are the main reasons I love my apartment in Pacific Grove.

Oh there's a bunch of other reasons too. But I can't discount the view. I can never discount the view.

In my few weeks of living on the Monterey Peninsula, I've been awed by the scenery at just about every turn. The beauty in this place just doesn't end. It gives everything an air of elegance.

Even the Army is more pleasant here. When you're at Ford Ord you can just look away from the drab colors and the heads without hair to see that beautiful bay glistening at the bottom of the hill.

Walk to any street corner and look down, then try to remember what's wrong with life.

I was outlining my awe to one of my new bosses here at *The Herald* the day I asked if I could get down and kiss the cornerstone of the newspaper building.

If I ever drive by the marina and fail to look over and notice how pretty the boats are in the water, it'll be time for me to move on, I said.

No, the boss said. If you ever overlook the beauty of that scene it will be time for us to move you on.

Damn, I hate to say this about bosses, but she's right. This place is just too gorgeous to be ignored.

Oh, yeah, if you're keeping score, the boss said I *could* kiss the cornerstone if I wanted to.

But I think I decided to save the kisses for some of my new neighbors.

Yes, I lucked out. A stunning view AND good neighbors. Now that's a combination most apartment dwellers only long for.

I've never found the combination before, not in a rental. But then, I've never lived on the Peninsula before.

Let me tell you about some of those new neighbors.

The two young women upstairs are bartenders. They live with a 4-year-old boy who is friendly, and a Labrador retriever who eats anything but onions.

One works down the street and one works in Carmel, which means there are already two bars where I can tarry with the knowledge that somebody in there will remember where I live. That could provide a freedom all its own.

I met the bartenders and the boy and the dog the day I moved in. It took about two minutes to know we'll get along just fine. We swapped notes on who sleeps where and generally when, so we haven't had a problem with stereos too loud at the wrong time or typing in the wrong part of the house or anything like that.

There are other neighbors too who seem all right, but I haven't gotten to know them so well. Which is perfect. We can be cordial on the street and wave through the windows and watch out for each others' cars but still go on about our own businesses.

A lot of the people on the block are connected to the bed-and-breakfast inn on the corner. They pass back and forth most of the day and always speak, usually to offer an observation about the weather or somebody's comings and goings. They make the street really neighborhoody.

Did I mention the inn gets as much as $185 a night for a room?

That's the inn three doors down.

That's $185 a night for the setting I'm worried about taking for granted.

Damn I like living here.

The guy next door doesn't work for the inn. He works out of his house. He's set up an office in the bay window next to mine in order to take full advantage of the view. I get to watch him work on his computer sometimes while I'm writing. Or while I'm sitting and looking at the boats and the divers and the waves.

I've talked to him about the view we share and how it inspires us. Mostly it inspires us to work hard enough to pay the rent.

Did I mention that gorgeous views aren't cheap?

But such a view is a continual reward for going through the hassles of finding it and financing it. I mean, this *was* the 39th apartment I looked at last month when I moved down from Sacramento,.

And the amount of rent I was willing to pay went up with every broken screen and every scarred wall I saw. Now I may not be able to afford to go out anymore. But with this view of Lovers Point, I may not need to.

One day I talked to the guy next door about the old houses we live in and how they were built. A lot of people in Pacific Grove talk houses like that. For a lot of reasons, of course. For starters, there are houses worth talking about in Pacific Grove.

There are tours of the old Victorians that I don't fully understand yet. But I stopped at the Chamber of Commerce office one day and picked up a brochure that outlines a tour of the old houses and places of interest in town. The brochure lists the addresses of 14 specific houses worth seeing. And, yes, one of them is the house I live in.

There are even more reasons the place makes me happy. Yeah, I know, a stunning view, good neighbors, charm and a sense of history should be more than enough. But just wait 'til you read this: The inside of the place was just rebuilt.

The apartment is almost as gorgeous as the view through the windows. The landlord did it himself and took a lot of time to restore the woodwork and floors. Then he put Victorian-styled wallpaper in every room, even the bathroom. He added some stained glass windows and brought a marble fireplace down from San Francisco.

And just as important, he rewired it so that there are plenty of electrical outlets for the stereos and VCRs and lamps and blenders that didn't exist 104 years ago. The plumbing is new too, with faucets that have pressure for the water.

Of course, the floors are cockeyed. That's 10 decades of wear and settling, I guess. My typewriter rolls away from me. My television rolls towards me. The bookcase leans away from the wall. The lamp leans into it.

Even with the movement, my furniture fits perfectly in the apartment. That's the furniture that overflowed from the biggest truck U-Haul rents, the furniture that lost all of its value in the pains and aggravations of moving it.

But a lot of it is Victorian antique, stuff I've collected for 20 years as indulgences, souvenirs, investments, inheritances and just functional furniture. The volume and variety seem perfect for this apartment. Even the colors are good.

Of course, I haven't unpacked everything yet. I'm still walking through a forest of cardboard boxes, wondering which one the ice cube trays are in.

I'm getting to things as I can.

And I think I've just decided that my record collection is unsuited for this setting. I'm heavy on Waylon Jennings and that ilk. But I think this place may be more appropriate for Johann Strauss and the boys.

96

Avoiding the Bells and Chimes of P.G.

This is almost embarrassing. But I'm having an unabashed love affair with the Monterey Peninsula.

In my first month or so of living here, I can find nothing seriously wrong with it.

Oh, I know I will eventually. But please give me the moment. Or the day or the week or the month or the year.

Right now I'm feeling like a tourist who doesn't have to check the oil and go home on Sunday afternoon.

The gorgeous views still awe me. And now I'm learning how livable this place really is.

Life is pretty convenient here. I think that may be a function of size. After all, this is a one-freeway peninsula.

Or it may be the result of living in Pacific Grove, which is a compact little town that has most things you need pretty handy.

Or it may result from working in downtown Monterey, another compact place that seems to be dominated by matters of commerce and lunch.

Such compactness means you don't have to spend a lot of time driving from one place to another.

Unless, of course, you get too close to the tourists who always turn left from the right-hand lanes, go the wrong way down one-way streets and park at green lights to double-check their maps.

But the generally quick trips in the car holds down the frustration and gives you time to admire the scenery.

I lucked out on that. It's only six minutes between my apartment in Pacific Grove and my job in Monterey, a short trip between two different worlds. Unless of course, you get stuck behind the tourists.

Midway, there's a two-block strip of Lighthouse Avenue that has all the stuff you need right away in a new home — grocery stores, gas stations, dry cleaners, video rentals. I can catch them coming or going, three minutes in either direction.

That's helping the livability. It's also helping me settle in. And not a minute too soon.

I've become quite tired of the chaos of moving. I'm past due to start playing on the Peninsula.

Besides, I'm going buggy with the bells in Pacific Grove.

Yes, bells.

I don't know where they come from, but every 15 minutes there are bells and chimes that break through the breeze to help mark time. They are delightful.

But I'm still new enough that I haven't figured out all the sounds of my apartment. So every time I'm home and hear the bells, I just automatically walk to the front door to see who's there.

It's one of those things I'll figure out someday.

But that can wait too, along with the unpacked boxes and the postal forms I haven't used to tell everybody my new address. I'm ready to get out of that apartment for a while. There's a whole new world that needs sampling.

Already I've found one favorite place — the bike trail, that strip of asphalt that sort of borders Monterey Bay.

I found the Pacific Grove end of the Recreation Trail, as it's called on government signs, just a block or so from my apartment. And off I went.

The view, and I'm sorry I can't think of better words, is absolutely stunning. The cypress at Lovers Point, the hills across the bay, the city in the distance, the aquarium that looks like a bank vault sitting out of place on the shoreline.

The ride is not fast and smooth, however, because of all the people walking on the trail and all the baby buggies.

Of course, the crunch is behind Cannery Row, where half the tourists in California like to stand around on the asphalt trail all at once, pretending they've forgotten how to take another step.

It was behind Cannery Row one day that I realized tourists have a common look: 50 pounds of belly poking through an ugly shirt and hanging down towards pasty legs shaped like fire plugs. Nothing embarrasses some people.

But I must say my observations might be skewed. They were cut short on the first run when a pedal of my brand-new, fancy, 18-speed mountain bike fell off on the clogged trail. And that, after I took so long to accept the fact that fancy bikes don't have fenders anymore. But pedals? Even I know better.

So I found a friendly bike repairman in Pacific Grove, who assured me that the people in the shop where I bought my brand-new, fancy, 18-speed mountain bike didn't know what they were doing when they put it together.

But he saved me.

I never before that day realized that bike repairmen are like dentists: they can find nothing acceptable in the work of their predecessors.

But the skilled bike repairman fixed my pedal and got me back on the trail before sunset.

The scenery was instantly refreshing, as always.

But a mile later, the same-looking tourists were clogging the trail.

After that, the trail itself began to get interesting.

It crosses some busy streets and cuts from asphalt to dirt for the next mile and a half, while it stretches beside the Presidio and the marina and the statue of Santa Rosalia, the patron saint who watches over the Italian fishermen in Monterey. Then the trail ends abruptly, right at the parking lot of Fisherman's Wharf.

There are no markings about it, no directions. But in time, a sandy-haired lad named Brill might find you looking silly and lead you through the auto and camper traffic in the parking lot, down a short street and across a sidewalk where the trail resumes.

I'm sure that someday I'll be annoyed enough about riding a bike through a busy parking lot to call that stupid planning. But for now, I think it's quaint.

It may be a diversion of dumb, but once out of it you're beside the state beach, that crescent of sand that sits behind the car lots of Del Monte Avenue, and the beauty takes over again.

Here is a lesson in why it's good to have a mountain bike along the ocean: you have 18 gears to shift down into when the wind picks up and hits you like a mountain. Gee, I'd call it good planning except now I know the shop I bought the brand-new, fancy, 18-speed mountain bike from is no good. Luck, I guess.

Soon you're protected from the wind, as you ride through eucalyptus stands with their always-fresh scent, past sand dunes that have well-worn paths in the iceplant, right next to the signs that say it's federal property and you should keep off.

It's stimulating again. Until, 4½ miles from Lovers Point, the bike trail ends, right at a K Mart.

I'm sure I'll consider that another stroke of stupid planning. But right now, that seems quaint too. And it keeps me away from the cardboard boxes and the bells of Pacific Grove.

He Had Everything
But a Phone Book

I think it's the phone company that started the trouble.

I always think it's the phone company that starts the trouble.

Except sometimes when it's an insurance company. Or a banker.

But this time it was definitely Pacific Bell that messed up my life.

It's just a simple thing, really. The phone company didn't send me a telephone book.

I've called them three times since it was supposed to have been delivered a month ago. I've offered to go down to the Monterey office to speed things up.

But no, the phone company has its own ways of doing things. So I have no phone book.

Sure, it's no big deal in the face of world situations and real problems. But it's damned inconvenient. Especially for someone who has just moved to the Peninsula and needs to look up the phone number of restaurants and doctors, the addresses of insurance offices and bicycle shops.

Have you ever dialed 411 and asked the operator to tell you the addresses of the State Farm Insurance offices in the book so you can see which one is closest to your new apartment? Try it.

Also stop at a phone booth or two and see if there's a phone book there you can use. If you find a booth with a book, report it. It's a natural for a believe-it-or-not item.

While you're there, see if by any chance the phone works. That could make it a really special day.

Okay, so I'm edgy and angry. Don't let me blow this inconvenience out of proportion. I still feel like I've found heaven here. It's just that I had forgotten you sometimes have to jiggle the key to get the door unlocked.

Bits of reality have started to work themselves into my new life. It seems not everybody in this paradise is as happy to have me here as I am.

Take the bank.

Ha! I have a new one.

I didn't plan to switch from Wells Fargo, which has been a fine bank for the past 10 years. After all, banking in California is slick enough that when you move from one place to another, a simple appearance at a new branch will change the addresses on your accounts, get you new checks and so on. Really easy. Supposedly.

But I went into the Wells Fargo branch in downtown Monterey on a lunch hour to change my address. I sat for seven minutes in the new-accounts section, being ignored by the five clerks working on ledgers and phones there. I got another case of edgy and angry and left.

If you can't get a bank's attention when you're trying to open an account, how in hell can you expect service when you've got a troubled check to deal with?

I think I found my answer: I switched to First Interstate Bank.

What a world of difference. I walked into First Interstate's branch in Pacific Grove one morning and all three new-accounts clerks asked to help me. Within 10 seconds I was sitting at a desk, listening to Diane Lugo explain the various fees, the check designs available, the mechanics of the plastic card.

It felt so homey in there, I'm thinking about opening a Christmas Club account.

The bank move ended happily, even without a phone book. But some other adjustments to the Peninsula haven't been as pleasant.

Cable television, for instance.

This is my first encounter with the cable. Rabbit-ear antennaes have been good enough everywhere else I've lived.

And after what I think is a fair and sufficient test, I find it to be just as crummy as free TV.

And I think it's overpriced.

It costs me $32.85 a month for 24 channels that seem to be dominated by black-and-white reruns and things for sale.

I'm not much of a television buff anyway, but this system makes me sorry I didn't accept a friend's offer to tap into a neighbor's cable and save the $32.85 a month.

In fairness, let me tell you there's one value — ONE — that I have found on Monterey Peninsula TV Cable: One of the channels carries "Nightline," which Ted Koppel turns into the finest news show on television. The ABC affiliate pre-empts it for "Divorce Court."

I catch "Nightline" about twice a week, which is about eight times a month, which is about $4.10 a shot. I could probably get the transcript from ABC for the price of postage.

Okay, okay. You really want to know what burns me about cable? It's 24 channels and not a single one of them carries "Rockford Files" reruns. That's an outrage the FCC should jump into.

Naturally I don't mind picking on cable. It's sort of like a new phone company.

But other media have given me moving problems, too.

Magazines come to mind. Some of them don't have forms in them to tell you the procedure for changing your mailing address so you can avoid forwarding postage.

Some of them do have those forms, of course. But some of those forms don't have places for the mailing labels off the front covers, the labels don't come off readily and some of the labels are bigger than the spaces allowed for them on the forms.

I wonder if anybody in a magazine subscription department has ever actually subscribed to one.

Or is this just another business attitude that flourishes in the Reagan years?

One of my favorite experiences on this move was with *Mother Jones,* a socialist magazine put out in San Francsico. If you don't know the magazine, it's usually a rag-tag production that looks like the work of a bunch of drunken sophomores. But sometimes it does some terrific reporting and breaks a story that blossoms into a national scandal when the big sheets pick up on it. I like to support that kind of work.

But the magazine has no form for you when you want to change mailing addresses. So I sent *Mother Jones* a post card. and somebody in that office sent me back a post card, personally written, to say the magazine has changed its address so would I please send them another post card to *their* new address, so they could properly record *my* new address.

See what I mean?

I hate to be so political, now that my college days are behind me. But I think maybe somebody has to be in charge sometimes or we'll never get our addresses coordinated.

Sorry, *Mother Jones.*

Of course, I might have called the magazines to tell them of my new mailing address. BUT I DON'T HAVE A PHONE BOOK to look up their numbers or area codes.

The book has to come all the way from Merced, if the erroneously deregulated phone company ever gets around to mailing it.

And, you know, it just occurred to me that I haven't had a phone bill for a good long time. I wonder if Pacific Bell is going to try to charge me for the information calls I've had to make.

Or, worse yet, will the phone company try to charge for the three extra calls I've made to ask for my book? Which, of course, I NEVER GOT!

Savoring the Peninsula
— A Bite at a Time

I feel like I've been eating my way through the Peninsula.

The extra pounds I've put on in the six weeks or so that I've been here are a clue, the pounds have pushed my belt out yet another notch.

And I seem to spend a lot of time picking restaurants, then getting to them and sitting around in them. That seems to have become my main recreation.

Some of it, of course, is just part of the chaos of moving. It takes time to unpack all the boxes that are sitting in front of the stove.

Some of it is due to all the visitors who have dragged through since

I've moved to a place they like. A steady stream of company has been forcing me to eat out a lot, partly because it's keeping me from unpacking the boxes of cooking utensils that are hiding the stove.

But I've also wanted to sample the restaurants because it's a natural way to explore my new home. Expensive, but natural.

When you stop and think about it, most newcomers meet their new towns through its restaurants.

You have to eat. And before you're settled in enough to cook, you can either bore yourself with fast food or eat out. And out. And out. And out.

I just sat here and tallied and surprised myself to see that I've already eaten in 44 different restaurants on the Peninsula. Damn, that's something like a different one each day. No wonder my belt has been growing.

The number does surprise me. And so do some of the things I've learned from such caloric exposure to the Peninsula.

For example, this place is hamburger crazy.

They put hamburger in everything here, even omelettes and salads.

Yes, the staid-looking, little restaurant near my apartment in Pacific Grove — right on the quaintest strip of the quaint, little town — is little more than a front for a hamburger stand.

Honest, this charming Victorian house has become a glorified McDonalds' with a menu that features dozens of varieties of hamburgers.

There is home-made soup on the menu too, which can be ordered as a first course to justify the stiffer price of a disguised Big Mac.

A lot of places that aren't so heavy on hamburger do the same thing with squid, usually fried.

There are a lot of menus on the Peninsula that feature squid and eggs for breakfast, squid and lettuce for lunch, squid and fried potatoes for dinner.

Then, of course, there are the carry-out cartons that contain fried squid for snacks. Or seal food.

Now don't get me wrong, I like squid. It's one of my favorite foods. Like hamburger.

Why, there's a squid house on Lighthouse Avenue that I used to dream about. I discovered it on a sort-of honeymoon 15 years ago, when I was a tourist from New York. I thought the place was wonderful, the calamari divine, and I've gone out of my way to get back to it once in a while since then.

But now that I live here and have been able to eat in that restaurant regularly, I've decided it's really not all that good. It's just kind of ordinary.

That's okay, mind you. But I've found notably better restaurants among the 43 others I now know about.

Actually, I've only found a few really crappy restaurants here. And that surprises me too, since so many places are tourist-oriented and don't need to rely on repeat business.

That's not to say most restaurants I've been to are really good. Most of them are pretty ordinary and rather bland. But even that is a higher standard that I expected in such a resort area.

In the 44 Peninsula restaurants I've sampled I've had only four truly awful meals. Which is something like 10 percent. Which is surprising for a resort.

And two of those crummy meals were edible, just regrettable.

In Marina I found a Chinese restaurant that actually put ketchup right into the wok as it stir-fried the broccoli. Yes, that's as disgusting as it sounds.

In Seaside I found a restaurant that uses ham that's so salty you have to drink water for three days just to wash the taste back into your mouth.

In Monterey I found some finger-licking garbage at a chicken stand that simply didn't cook the meat to the bone.

And on Cannery Row I found one of the few meals I've ever left sitting on a restaurant table. They called it fried squid, but it was so overcooked in dirty grease that it could have been anything from fried shoestrings to battered gull droppings.

Actually, I could have seen that one coming if I'd have scouted a little better. It was the dining room of one of the heaviest advertisers on Cannery Row.

The advertising volume doesn't necessarily mean anything, but the ads themselves would have been a clue. This place advertises fettuccine and chicken teriyaki as seafood.

Most restaurant ads aren't so revealing. But they are plentiful here.

Motels on the Peninsula have lots of supposed guide books for tourists. The slickest one—named *The Visitors & Convention Guide, The Pocket Guide to the Monterey Peninsula*—lists 12 places to eat and recommends them with words like fine, elegant, creative and gourmet. Coincidentally, the 12 restaurants on the recommended list are the same 12 that bought ads in the little carry-along guide.

I haven't done a guide book of my own yet, schlock or otherwise. But I have already found some favorite places worth going back to again and again.

Do you want my list? Remembering that I've eaten at nearly four times as many places as listed in the slickest guide book handed out at motels?

Okay, here's my top 10, so far:

Rio Grill in the Crossroads shopping center in Carmel, by far my favorite food on the Peninsula so far, including squash soups and an inventive version of liver and onions.

Beau Thai Restaurant, upstairs at 807 Cannery Row, a Thai restaurant that's as charming as it is good, with some of the best food bargains in town.

Whaling Station Inn Restaurant at 763 Wave St., pricey but terrific seafood.

First Watch, a patio-oriented restaurant at 125 Ocean View Blvd., Pacific Grove, that provides the best breakfasts I've found on the Peninsula. I'm especially partial to the Pope John — a Polish sausage with eggs that have mushrooms, onions and Swiss cheese in them, potatoes on the side and an English muffin — for $4.95.

Peppers, a Mexican-type restaurant at 170 Forest Ave., Pacific Grove, good because it serves Cuban black beans with its meals instead of cheese-saturated refrieds.

Rosine's Restaurant at 434 Alvarado St., Monterey, which has the best salads and breads I've found so far.

Old Monterey Cafe at 489 Alvarado St., which features fancy hamburgers.

Troia's Market at 350 Pacific St., Monterey, for strictly carry-out from the best delicatessen in town.

Sandbar & Grill overlooking the Monterey marina on Municipal Wharf No. 2. This is a recommendation with reluctance because the Sandbar food is okay, but not great. The price is OK, but not cheap. It is the view that is terrific. But watch out for the breakfasts they misname as brunch.

Scotch Bakery at 545 Lighthouse Ave., Pacific Grove. Sure it's not a restaurant. But it gets on my top-10-so-far list because it makes the best pastries I've found in my 42 years of life. And if you think that's stretching an idea, you can always do your own list.

A Day   In Sausalito

Suffering Homesickness
in Sausalito

The Monterey Peninsula can ruin you in a hurry.

I hadn't lived here two months when I left for my first weekend out of town. I went to a wedding in Sausalito, that quaint little town on the other end of the Golden Gate Bridge that's so neat people pay thousands of dollars just to get there, then hundreds more each day to stay.

I used to think it was worth that. I've always been enchanted by the views of and from Sausalito, its civility and its general attitude that life is charming if you can afford it.

But that was before I lived here.

On this trip, I thought Sausalito was nothing more than OK. It's nice, sure. But it's no Monterey.

I missed my new home more than I thought I would, even though I was gone for just a weekend and I was among some of my closest friends for a two-day party.

I think I missed the sea otters at Lovers Point most.

Or maybe it was just the view.

The San Francisco skyline is certainly stunning, the bay gorgeous, the Golden Gate Bridge awesome and the Oakland Bay Bridge beautiful. But that panorama just doesn't have the freedom in it that I see in Monterey Bay.

I think it's the bridges — or the lack of a wake or maybe the imposition of the skyline itself — but the San Francisco Bay from Sausalito seems to be a lake, not part of the ocean. It's like a gigantic pond, closed in and controlled on all sides. It seems like something you'd put a paddle boat on.

I missed the surf. And the waves breaking on the rocks. And beaches. And the openness of the sea, without a bridge in sight.

I tried very hard not to be critical of Sausalito. After all, it really is a nice town. And I was trying especially hard to be polite because a bunch of people had come from far away — Sacramento, Los Angeles, Ohio, China and Saudia Arabia — to take part in a wedding, not to hear my unsolicited observations about the California coast.

But several bottles of champagne later and I wasn't so polite.

I was homesick!

Let's fact it, newcomers to Monterey can become as zealous in their worship as converted Catholics. Or reformed smokers.

Eventually, I had to point out to the wedding crowd that Monterey Bay is simply prettier than San Francisco Bay.

Moss Landing smokestacks in the distance don't make it seem as finite as the one defined by one of the world's most spectacular skylines.

The Peninsula coastline also provides more access to the actual water. In Sausalito it seemed like the bay was always on the other side of a stone wall or behind the locked fences of marinas that block the view with dozens of boats that belong to somebody else. It was a lot like the suburbs moved to a lakefront.

And I was a general bore about the whole thing, several bottles of champagne into it. If this marriage doesn't work out, I probably won't be invited back to any future weddings. Unless, of course, I'm living in Fresno or Bakersfield or some other place I wouldn't care to talk about.

But the Peninsula has simply raised my expectations. Already.

In just a weekend, I missed Monterey enough that I started reading Steinbeck, ordered calamari for dinner and left Sausalito ahead of schedule in order to get back and take a ride along the ocean.

I think I see why so many people here vacation in Europe and exotic places in the South Pacific. It's just damned hard to beat what we live with every day.

It's funny that a place can be so spectacular it makes a town as neat as Sausalito seems like a curio. A lovely curio, to be sure, but just not the treat it used to be.

It has fog and gulls and sailboats. And it has room rents just as high as the Monterey Peninsula. It was warmer there. And the food was noticeably better in Sausalito, with *ripe* fruit and plenty of chicken dishes. Of course the water in the tap was better.

The Monterey Bay has freedom in it. It has the surf, waves breaking on the rocks. Beaches. And the openness of the sea, without a bridge in sight.

But there were no playful sea otters. Or ground squirrels scampering about.

Believe it or not, I also missed the tunnel down by Fisherman's Wharf. I don't know what it's called — Fisherman's Wharf Tunnel, Lighthouse Tunnel or just "the" tunnel. But I have yet to drive through it without at least one person honking a car horn to hear the echo.

And I think that's refreshing. It's such an honest and unsophisticated way to take part in the world around you, a very simple pleasure.

I can imagine sea otters honking car horns in tunnels.

And I can imagine them never wanting to leave Monterey Bay, even for a weekend.

But maybe you have to get away once in a while to appreciate what you've got. It's kind of like going abroad to get a closer look at America, I guess. Or, yeah, like not missing the water until the well runs dry . . . Or

111

something like that.

I even missed the sale signs along Cannery Row. And the "discount" alerts and the "just arrived" notices.

There's one grand opening on the Monterey waterfront that's into its second year now. And I missed that sign, too.

All My Friends
Are Eager to Visit

I'm thinking about answering my phone here with "Bay View Bed and Breakfast" instead of my usual "Uh-hello."

It seems like most of the calls I'm getting now that I live on the Monterey Peninsula are from people who want to come and visit.

Some of them are close friends who are always welcome, of course. But some of the calls are from people I hardly know who say it's time for us to get together for a weekend and wouldn't I like to meet the wife and kids?

Guess where they think the meeting should be.

It's getting kind of crazy. The numbers are overwhelming me and keeping me from exploring this place at my own pace, on my own whims. Most of the visitors want to see and do the same things, over and over and over.

That's not boring, mind you. I've established a Tour One that leaves from my apartment at Lovers Point, wanders along the ocean to 17-Mile Drive, stops for leg stretches at Fanshell Beach, Cypress Point and the fenced-off Lone Cypress overlook, wanders on to Carmel Bay where the car gets parked so the tour group can hit the public toilets on the beach before walking up the hill to roam in and out of the shops. And get an ice cream. Then it's on to Carmel Mission and back to the apartment, via Highways 1 and 68, to get ready to go out to dinner.

The mission is always the last stop on the prime tour because it makes me angry. I know this will be considered sacrilegious by many, but I find elements of racism at Carmel Mission that offend me.

Yes, the mission is beautiful and generally inspirational. But it has a sign in the graveyard that numbers the 2,364 Indians buried there. It has a bigger sign in a garden on the other side of the church that salutes four Eastern settlers buried there, names them and calls them honorable.

This offends me because I'm part Indian. Since I've become an adult and figured some things out, I find it impossible to accept any form of racism or to act like it's OK.

I'm sure the Indians buried at the mission had names, too. And I'm sure most of them were honorable, just as I'm sure most of them were probably mistreated by white settlers.

What would I do if I were the bishop? I'd remove the damned sign that honors the settlers. Or I'd post the names of 2,364 native Californians buried in the cemetery.

Then I'd put signs on the granite mortars that are used as decorations on the mission grounds. The signs would say these aren't ashtrays, so don't put your butts here unless you put cigarette ashes in the blenders and food processors in contemporary kitchens.

With those changes, people like me could visit the mission happily and feel welcome to think the place is beautiful and inspirational, not bigoted.

See why I make that the last stop before dinner? And dinner always starts with a few drinks.

Which doesn't seem to offend the many visitors I've had on the Peninsula. *Nothing* seems to offend them.

It took me a while to figure out what was happening with all the company. I didn't realize some people were just looking for a way to visit paradise without paying rent until the weekend I said sorry, I'm not going to be in town. That's OK, the want-to-be-visitors on the phone said. Just leave your apartment key some place where we can find it.

Then there were the people who said OK, if the weekends are booked we'll just change our vacation plans and stay with you during the week.

It was somewhere in there — when I had four families visiting in a 10-day period — that I decided I needed some rules.

I was dragging into work tired from all the company and late nights. I was putting on weight with all the dinners out and no time to exercise. And I was getting a little confused because I didn't have time to catch up with the paperwork of life, like balancing the checkbook and figuring out who I had to pay when.

I was getting a little desperate for some time to myself. Hell, I had so little time free I hadn't memorized my new phone numbers or the secret codes of my new bank cards and I still had to carry notes about them.

I'm sure it's happened to everyone who has moved here from less-than-a-resort, like the Sacramento I came from.

But I honestly hadn't thought it all through in advance, when I was running around at going-away parties inviting everyone to come visit.

Oh, I knew some pals would be down for the Jazz Festival. And I expect a sizable group for Thanksgiving. That's tradition.

But I really didn't expect the flood that has overwhelmed me.

So I called some friends who moved to San Diego a year or so ago and asked them how they handle all the visitors. They just lie, they said, and tell people they've already got company for any particular weekend.

It may have to come to that. But right now I'm being honest and just telling folks that I need some time to myself.

I haven't had a nap since I've been here. I haven't read much. I haven't been to the beach enough. And I haven't utilized the Home Box Office that I'm paying at least $14 a month for. (I think HBO is more than that, but the cable television bill is such a tangle I haven't been able to figure out exactly what costs what.)

Friends accept the truth.

And the people that don't care about your schedule and needs react kind of funny when you live in a resort. They don't hang up in anger when you tell them to stay away. They bargain.

Here's one that just called. Her boyfriend is going to be gone for a weekend, so she decided to come down and visit me. No.

Well, maybe just for one night. No.

She wouldn't even intrude. She could be in and out without my knowing she was ever here. No.

Well, call if you change your mind. OK.

See how easy this can be?

After all, I didn't move to this paradise to become the newest innkeeper on the Peninsula. I didn't die and go off to run a guesthouse.

Now I'm Living With the Rich and Famous

It was Kim Novak that I really wanted to meet. I mean, *really* wanted to meet.

Like a lot of American men my age, I've had a crush on her for maybe 30 years. It was a movie camera that burned a vision of her seductive eyes and soft blonde hair into my psyche. It was my puberty at the time that kept it there.

She was luscious. And my first real lust.

Kim Novak — and her scenes in the movie "Bell, Book and Candle" — caused me to give up a baseball card collection and my BB gun because I no longer had time for such childish things.

I was too preoccupied with our secret romance, an affair that amounted to me buying a bunch of cheesey magazines that had her picture on the covers, sorting through them for hours and covering the walls of my room with the best of the bunch.

Relationships like that change as you get on with life, but you never quite get over them.

I admit I've even judged women in my adult life and criticized them because they didn't measure up to Kim Novak . . . and what we once had together.

I've also sought her out a few times, even recently.

A few years ago I heard or read that she lived in the Monterey area, somewhere around Big Sur, running a goat farm or something like that.

So the next time I vacationed here I went even more slowly along Highway 1, looking carefully at the coastal hills for something that looked like a goat farm.

Then I tarried for hours at the little store in Big Sur hoping Kim might stop in for some wheat germ or some writing pencils. Or to sell some homemade cheese or something.

No luck and no luck.

So last year I tried a more reasonable approach — I called her booking agent in Los Angeles and asked for an interview.

Now there's only one aside that I need to tell you about and it is this:

I was in Sacramento at the time, working for a newspaper named the Bee. The bosses had just transferred me to the staff of the paper's Sunday magazine, a move considered a treat for generally hard-nosed reporters like I had become. At the magazine the staff wanted fresh ideas, so I suggested some celebrity interviews which we hadn't done for years. I suggested a lot of names, but only two of them aroused universal interest in the room full of magazine people — Chuck Berry and Kim Novak. Everybody wondered about both of them. But the men on the staff, all in their early and mid-40s, got the same drifty look in their eyes that I had when we talked about *our* Kim.

Well, her agent turned us down.

As did Chuck Berry's, for that matter.

And then, as I've said before, I moved to the Monterey Peninsula. And now I'm sort of neighbors with Kim Novak.

I haven't actually met her, mind you, but I've met people who have. And they tell me she's active in Peninsula life so it's probably just a matter of time before I encounter her at one event or another.

Ho, ho, ho! A comfortable home with one of the most beautiful views in the world and now this!

Heaven has no fences!

I've already seen pictures of Kim Novak on the society pages of *The Herald,* taking part in a fashion show in Carmel. Ah, how beautiful she looked.

I've seen other celebrities pictured and named on those pages too, celebrities I don't care so much about because they weren't important to me in puberty, but celebrities who make this place feel that much more delightful because we've chosen to share it.

Just in the couple of months that I've lived here I've seen coverage of my new neighbors like Hank Ketcham, the Dennis the Menace cartoonist whose work made me open up the newspaper when I was a kid. Merv Griffin, Eva Gabor, Paul Anka. Doris Day and Reggie Jackson live around here somewhere too, I hear.

And, of course, there's Clint Eastwood.

It is Eastwood that I intended to tell you about today. Kim Novak just sort of jumped to the front of my mind and I got a little carried away. Thanks.

But here's what I wanted to tell you about Clint Eastwood.

The mayor of Carmel is such a celebrity that I rarely get through a day on the Peninsula without hearing his name at least once. Sometimes it's in conversation (as in, "Well, Clint told me that . . ."), sometimes on television (as in movie promos and previews) and sometimes just on the street (as in tourists who ask, "Hey, buddy, where's Clint's bar . . . house . . . office?").

There is such a Clint Eastwood presence here that I've often wondered which name is more exploited, Eastwood or John Steinbeck.

But I have to admit I took a visitor into the mayor's Hog's Breath Inn one night because she wanted to see this world-famous bar.

It looked like a Hollywood casting-call in there. Beautiful young women sat gazing at the door. Muscular young men paraded throughout the cafe. And gazed at the door.

We felt old enough and fat enough in there that we left without a drink or a closer look. We went on down the street where a neighbor who is the bartender could console us.

I don't know what I expected from the mayor's bar really. Which may be why it wasn't my idea to go in there.

And I don't know what I expected from the mayor himself, who I met recently when the mayors of Peninsula cities gathered to endorse candidates in the Nov. 3 election.

I had heard Eastwood was a nice guy, although a guy with his movie image as a toughie isn't expected to be. And an actor with his box office power certainly doesn't have to be.

I had also heard that he was sincere about being the mayor of Carmel and kept himself informed about even the most mundane municipal matters.

But I have to admit, when I met Eastwood we didn't talk much about sewers and curbs and things like that. I asked him about his celebrity status and how he deals with it and whether he likes it. (He said it's OK when you want to get a table down front. But generally, he said, he's a private person who likes to travel alone.) And then he asked me about a reporter I used to work with, *The Herald*'s fight for a document from the regional water district and how I was liking my new life on the Peninsula.

Frankly, I was charmed. Twenty years of hard-nosed reporting went to hell for a few minutes while I talked to a movie star about human things.

I found Eastwood to be gracious, polite, warm, maybe even a little reticent in the half-hour or so I was around him. Maybe that kind of humanity is doubly impressive because you don't really expect it in a star of his magnitude.

As we walked out of the hotel, Eastwood offered me a ride back to *The Herald* office. It was only a couple of blocks away, but I told him I'd love the ride if I could have bragging rights. How often does a household name offer you a ride to work?

He had cassette tapes on the front seat and T-shirts on the back, just like most of us. And his car, which I don't want to pinpoint, looked just like any of 2,000 others you might see on the streets of Carmel. It had standard license plates on it, simply the next number in the sequence that came off the line at Folsom Prison.

There was nothing about the car — or Eastwood's manner or conversation or gray, pin-striped suit — that suggested anything but nice.

When I stepped out I had to resist the urge to tell him that he had made my day. He must hear versions of that Dirty Harry line a thousand times a week. A few seconds on film that he'll have to live with forever.

I wonder if that's what Kim Novak has to go through, from guys who saw "Bell, Book and Candle" in puberty.

The Best Things
In Life Are Free

Housing is the only outrageous cost I've found in paradise.

Housing and the telephone, that is.

Housing and the telephone and cable television, actually.

Housing and the telephone and cable television and restaurants, if you want the whole list.

But that's the only outrageous cost I've found since I moved to the Monterey Peninsula a couple of months ago.

Well, maybe parking tickets, too.

Sometimes I feel like I'm buying the streets of Monterey and paying for them $10 at a time.

This is all fresh in my mind because I've just paid my monthly bills and found that I had to stall one — the $100 phone bill.

Now that's not a new experience, of course. There have been periods in my life where I sort of expected thank you notes for getting my payments in on time. Or reasonably close to time.

But I've gotten more responsible since then and I've generally downscaled my lifestyle to adjust to my income and the lunacies of American economics.

A small apartment in paradise will do for me now, with an aging Japanese car, a wardrobe familiar in the '60s and a camera with just one lens.

Good wine and fine restaurants are about the only things I haven't been willing to scrimp on in my middle ages. Until I moved here.

Some of the restaurants might have to go.

I just can't keep spending more than I make. And I doubt I can convince my new bosses to do the right thing by my paycheck.

Now don't get me wrong. *The Herald* pays a fair wage for this kind of work. It's just not enough to support my tastes. Why, this is the sixth paper in a row that hasn't paid me enough.

It's an unpleasant fact that reporters are never rich. Which really isn't surprising, since rich people aren't hungry enough to go through the torment sometimes involved in getting information and making it public. People who can do that generally don't know how to promote themselves enough to get rich. Money and reporting are almost mutually exclusive.

That injustice aside, I'm trying to figure out how to live on the Peninsula without movie royalties, investment dividends or inherited wealth to clutter up my checking account.

It would be hard to cut my entertainment expenses because they are minimal, especially now that I "just say no" to would-be visitors from increasingly far-away places.

I've had no lavish parties here, no big dinner gatherings or cookouts and I haven't found a bar worth buying a round of drinks in.

I've only seen four movies since I've been here, and two of those were on television, if I remember right.

I don't think I've been to any concerts. The only tickets I recall were for the Monterey Jazz Festival — which were amazingly half-price from a scalper at the front gate — and the Monterey Bay Aquarium — which were strikingly overpriced for an educational institution.

The best entertainment here is the free stuff — the mesmerizing scenery and the ocean trails and the sunsets and the beaches and the sidewalks past pretty houses and the forests and the parks. Wow! What a spectacular place nature has provided.

And with the exception of automobile fees here and there, it's all free.

And wonderful.

The lesser things in life — like dry cleaning and gasoline and clothes and groceries and haircuts — are all pretty much the same price everywhere these days. The real Levis are $20 in Monterey or Sacramento or Chicago or New York. A gallon of gas is about a buck here or anywhere. A quart of milk is 60 cents all around the country. And a bottle of aspirin is within pennies of the same price on any shelf in America.

It's when you get away from the daily bread kind of stuff that you can find the price differences on the Peninsula.

Some things are actually cheaper here. Car insurance, for instance. My rates dropped from about $1,000 a year to $750 after I moved from Sacramento to Pacific Grove — and switched insurance companies.

Property insurance is harder to tell about. I couldn't get the same kind of coverage here that I had in Sacramento because insurance companies don't cater to renters' policies like they do to homeowners. The result is I'm paying $240 a year for less coverage than I wanted.

Medical insurance is hard to tell about, too. I have to pay $125 a month to fill in the gap between the group coverage at my old job and my new. It's a new expense for me, but I dont' know if it's high or low.

That medical insurance may actually prove to be worthwhile, though, because I seem to have developed a problem with my blood pressure. It makes no sense, but I seem to have hypertension here. How can there be stress in paradise?

At first I assumed it was just the stress of moving — seeing to a million details, saying a hundred goodbyes, living on fast food with too little time for proper exercise.

When the blood pressure didn't go down, I figured it was the press of the extra tonnage I've picked up in the past couple of months.

Then I thought it was the notable absence of good bars here.

But now I think maybe it's the strain of housing costs and trying to pay them.

I'm paying $800 a month plus utilities for a one-bedroom apartment that would rent for half that in Sacramento.

But, of course, you couldn't see the ocean from the living room window in that one.

Or walk three houses down and stand on a beach to watch the sea otters play.

Now that may be the way I like to live, whether I can afford to or not. But it's also one of the reasons my phone bill is so high.

I've got one of those little tape machines that answers the phone when I'm not home. Yes, I think they're less than wonderful too. But that little machine had been one of the most valuable tools in my life for years. Now that I live here, it's costing me a fortune.

Friends call from out of town, see, and leave messages on my tape. When I get home, I have to call them back. Of course, I pay the long-distance rates that way.

Some of the calls are fine and welcome. But some of the calls I have been paying to return are from people who want to know when they can come visit the seashore.

And watch my $37-a-month cable television.

Pity the Tourist
Lost in The Streets

I've come to feel sorry for the tourists here. I really have.

Even though they've driven me off the bike trail on Saturdays.

And they keep me out of Carmel and away from Fisherman's Wharf and Cannery Row on weekends.

And they take over my favorite beaches at Lovers Point just as if I wasn't here.

And they take up the parking spaces closest to my apartment.

And they walk by and stare into my window like I'm some kind of a museum display.

I really can accept all that. In my good moods. Because I know what we're giving back to them.

True, they are getting to look at some of the most beautiful scenery in the world.

Also true that they are getting to refresh themselves with that crisp, clean, ocean air.

But they have to pay Peninsula prices for that.

And they also have to cope with one of the silliest traffic patterns in the world. That's why I feel sorry for them.

Just look at some of the streets around here.

In Pacific Grove there are two-way streets that switch to one-ways right in the middle of a block. Take away a single street sign and you've got a headon collision with the kinds of liability questions that sleazy lawyers are just waiting for.

And there really isn't a surplus of signs anywhere.

I swear I lived here two months before I figured out how to get to the Monterey Conference Center and all the hotels around it from Del Monte Boulevard. And that's the street that runs right in front of it.

The problem is trying to follow the road as it runs in front of Fisherman's Wharf. The natural flow of the heavy traffic on Del Monte is to bend around the wharf and go through the tunnel toward Cannery Row and Pacific Grove. The sign directing you to veer left to stay downtown isn't obvious to a stranger.

Of course, coming in from the other side you can miss an abrupt sign about the tunnel and end up on Pacific Street, where there's nothing right away to tell you you're really within a few blocks of where you want to be and a series of left turns will get you there.

If you're in a sadistic mood some time, go down to the Presidio gate right there and watch all the U-turn attempts, the confused faces and the map-pulling-outs. Then watch oncoming motorists hit the brakes as they spot the confused motorists stopped in the intersection.

I've lived here long enough to figure out some things like that. But it took a lot of corrective driving to figure it out. There's any number of extra lefts and rights ground into my steering wheel. But I still get confused and lost almost daily. I've gone through three maps in three months.

I really do feel sorry for strangers who have to deal with that. We offer them tangles of triangles and Y-intersections and 135-degree turns, all mixed in with a confusing array of one-way and two-way traffic patterns, two-lane and three-lane streets and senseless zig-zags at almost every corner.

Consider this one:

The heavy traffic flowing down Munras Avenue from the freeway is suddenly confronted with a junction not clearly marked. Munras Avenue ventures off to the left and, after some dog's-hind-leg twists, becomes Jefferson Street.

But the natural flow of traffic is to ignore the jump to the left and just keep going straight toward the ocean, whether or not you know the street name will change to Abrego then Washington.

Of course, if you look at a map, you can see that Munras makes that poorly-marked left. Then it disappears.

You might not see that you should take the even-less-well-marked right twist onto Alvarado Street. But then Alvarado ends in a couple of blocks at Del Monte, where you have to turn left. Two blocks later, Del Monte ends at Van Buren, in what appears to be a residential area.

I think a map stand right at that corner would be an extremely profitable business.

My all-time favorite traffic puzzle is at that unnatural bend of Munras, where you have to get into the left lane to get through the Alvarado intersection, then you snap into the right lane to keep from being forced to turn left onto Calle Principal, then back to the left lane to keep from being forced to turn right on Pacific Street.

In the equivalent of a block, you have to change lanes three times in order to stay on the same street.

Throw a confused tourist or two into that stupidity and see who's late for work.

Now I've heard the explanation that the streets of Monterey were originally cow paths. The wandering cattle cut trails that were eventually paved over and called streets.

Maybe.

But I prefer to think these street patterns were intentional. Cows couldn't be this illogical.

I can see a couple of possibilities — a takeoff on a "Monty Python" routine, with the Minister of Silly Streets in charge; or a civilian job for a sadist who designed torture techniques to be used during the interrogation of enemy spies.

Then too, I won't discount the possibility that the streets of Monterey were laid out by participants in a drug rehabilitation program.

Clearly it's a cop-out to blame cows that have long since been smothered with potatoes and carrots.

What about the three different streets named Lighthouse Avenue, all in the same section of the Peninsula? Cows didn't do that, did they?

And what about that intersection where Munras and Pearl converge, along with Alvarado and Polk? Traffic blinded by buildings is forced into the path of vehicles that don't have stop signs. What about that?

Did a cow do that? A sadist? A silly person? Or a common drunk?

Something like two million tourists a year are thrown into those traffic patterns with little warning. Think about that and I think you'll feel sorry for them, too.

I can envision a day when thousands of boy scouts will be sent to the Peninsula to look for confused tourists to help them cross the streets.

Of course I may be more conciliatory than most Peninsula residents. But as a newcomer, it would be hypocritical for me to say that I'm here now, let's lock the gates.

Before I get too sympathetic, though, let me just make it clear that I don't always feel *that* sorry for the tourists.

Sometimes I envy them.

They seem to have the time to do all the things I want to do, but just haven't been able to get around to while working for a living.

They're always on the beaches. And walking along the ocean. And sitting at outdoor cafes. And exploring the forests. And wandering in and out of art galleries. And crowding into the aquarium.

Sometimes I take great pleasure in knowing that when they stop their leisurely meandering and wander back to their cars, they're probably going to find parking tickets on the windshields.

Life by the Bay
Gets Better and Better

I've lived three months by the bay and I can't imagine ever getting tired of it.

Part of me is starting to feel like I belong here. But I can't get over feeling privileged every time I look out my window and see the Pacific Ocean just rolling in and slapping at the rocks at the end of the street.

I am still awed when I walk along it, which is almost daily.

I'm not sure why the ocean is so soothing — the rhythm of the waves, the power of its size, the beauty of its colors, the freshness that blows in from it — but I know that it is.

And I've found that I can get a humble perspective on life within five minutes of ocean exposure, no matter how angry, frustrated or depressed I am. I think ocean walks could eliminate shrinks and cure alcoholics.

I also think the ocean is keeping me from exploring life on the Peninsula as quickly as I had assumed I would.

When I moved here three months ago to start working as The Herald's newest reporter, I intended to look into the nooks and crannies and find the bridges that may not be obvious here. I was going to be the fresh eye in the back yard.

I've done some of that, of course. But the pace has been slower than I expected.

Unpacking took a long time, partly because I was pre-occupied with the ocean three doors away.

I got submerged with visitors, partly because I was spreading the word about the proximity of the ocean.

I got more tied up with work than I expected, partly because I have to write a lot to cover the high costs of living along the water.

There was one lapse when a bug hit me and made me drop everything for a few days to sleep, watch television and eat sensibly.

There have been other setbacks when I got lonesome and homesick for particular people I left behind.

But mostly I've been running behind in my exploration because I have been hung up adoring the ocean.

I don't want to bore you with it, but I do want to tell you about one of the most remarkable scenes I've ever encountered.

It was right at Lovers Point one foggy afternoon. There was a slapping on the water, like somebody was hitting it with a big hand to make a "bam-bam" sound.

Naturally, I walked down to check it out. And there was what I know as a harbor seal — one of the slick-looking, black and white spotted critters — popping up out of the water and diving back down, slapping the surface with his tail each time to make the loud "ker-whack" sound.

The scene needed nothing but a popcorn vendor and ushers.

Now how can I leave things like that to go look for bridges? Or venture into Carmel Valley? Or try to figure out where Prunedale is?

Even when there's not a formal show going on, there's almost always a sea otter floating in the surf, slapping himself on the belly to make a milder "bam-bam" sound. I don't know why. But it's charming.

If it's not the critters in the water, it's the ground squirrels that poke in and out of that powdery soil just west of Lovers Point.

There are times when it's hard to walk on the trails through the gorgeous plants because of all the ground squirrels scampering about.

They're very domestic and super friendly and literally eat out of the hands that feed them. But so many people feed them so much stuff, most of the ground squirrels are fat.

When I first moved here, I just assumed all those little pudges were pregnant. Now that I've watched so many people feed them peanuts, sunflower seeds and bread crumbs, I understand the bellies that drag in and out of their holes in the ground.

I've decided not to feed the cute little animals. Instead, I'm looking for tiny collars and little straps so I can take them for walks along the beach.

I'd take them down to Asilomar to watch the sunsets that turn the horizon pink and purple and red and orange.

But before I get too carried away, let me take care of some business here.

This is the 13th installment of a newcomer's observations and experiences that we call "First Impressions."

They've been getting more attention than I expected, which is both flattering and bothersome.

I've had several dozen letters and cards and phone calls about my impressions. Enough to make me nervous. I'm used to dealing with news sources, not readers. Like most reporters, I'm really kind of shy.

A lot of the reaction has been from other newcomers, some of them just wanting to say "Hi" to one of their own.

Some has been from people wanting to direct a newcomer's attention to something in particular.

Only a few of the letters have been critical. And clearly wrong.

Some readers have offered me things. An invitation to join a couple on their honeymoon may be the most remarkable offer. But I've been asked on dates, too, by a half-dozen newcomer women.

And I've been invited to two parties, three home-cooked dinners, lunch and a concert. I've been offered free drinks, a free checking account, several telephone books, guides to Peninsula restaurants and help unpacking.

One thing I did get is worth recommending. It's a very good guide to Peninsula restaurants, a book called "Eating in Eden." It's a collection of thumbnail reviews of more than 180 restaurants around the Monterey Bay. It'll cost you $8.95, but if you eat out a lot, it's worth it.

And I'm not just saying that because the book is written by Patrick Franklin, a Herald critic who gave me a free copy. I'm saying it because it's an honest guide in which only six of the 180 restaurants are applauded as superb, some of the more famous places are put down as overrated.

There are also the readers who have offered corrections for things that seemed right to me at the time. I think column number 13 is the appropriate place to fix my mistakes. And here they are:

Correction 1: Sea otters don't bark, sea lions do.

Correction 2: "The Rockford Files" is on one of the cable channels.

Correction 3: The closest-to-a-local ABC affiliate doesn't cancel "Nightline" for "Divorce Court," it merely delays it until midnight.

Correction 4: All tourists are not fat.

Correction 5: I'm 43, not 42. At my age, it's easy to overlook the last birthday.

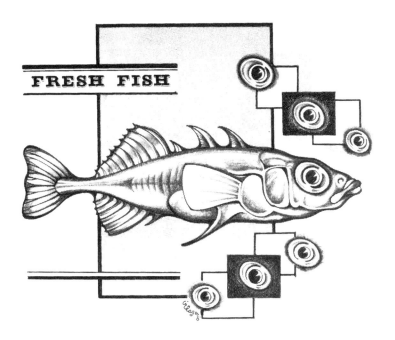

FRESH FISH

Eyeball-to-Eyeball
With Your Dinner

It's never been my idea of a good time, standing around a crowded market looking at dead fish.

In fact, it was one of those things I had managed to avoid for several months.

There have been enough other things to keep me busy in my new life on the Peninsula — washing windows, studying street maps, looking for parking places. Paradise does have its drudgeries.

Besides, I've never considered anything with eyes to be real food. Oh, I know, it would be silly to believe that all the cows and pigs and chickens that have gone into this gut have been blind. But I never had to look at any of their faces. The parts that I've seen came out of refrigerators, which is where food should come from.

But I had some company this weekend and they thought it would be fun to buy some fresh fish and cook it for dinner.

Before I get lost in my complaints, let me just say they were right. It was fun. And the food was wonderful. And I may never do it again.

It wasn't the walk down to Fisherman's Wharf — that was the best part. It was a beautiful day for a stroll along the ocean. Sunshine was everywhere and the surf was rolling in ever so gently. The sea otters were performing. And most of the people we passed between Lovers Point and Fisherman's Wharf were smiling and acting very happy with life.

Of course, I was chattering as if I really had something to say.

But somewhere in all the words I noticed that I have absorbed a number of names of places since I moved here. And I've picked up enough tidbits to have a sense of history.

It truly impressed my friends.

I pointed out that we were approaching China Point — or Point Cabrillo, depending on what map you want to use to see that the rock formation at Stanford University's Hopkins Marine Station has a name.

I dazzled them as we walked past Cannrey Row, explaining there are only a few of the original buildings left. A group of local business people and artists bought the actual Doc Ricketts lab to keep it from being torn down. The Hovden Cannery got serious infusions of cash to be preserved as the Monterey Bay Aquarium. An old brothel survives on ice cream sales today. And the last of the fisherman shanties are being allowed to rot out of the way.

I talked knowingly about the Coast Guard station and the marina, pointed out a boat I know and chattered about the rickety old buildings that stick out on the wharf.

And then I did it. I directed their attention to the Presidio and explained that was the site of an Indian village when the Spanish first landed in 1602. It was apparently called Tamokt by the native Californians, but the white sailors renamed the place after Spanish royalty. Monterey, I believe, means king's mountain or king's woods or something like that.

That's when I noticed how really impressed my friends were with all this local information. And, of course, they were trusting me for its accuracy. They weren't going to check any of it.

It occurred to me that you really wouldn't have to know much to impress visitors here. Toss in an Isabella Point once in a while or a

Clyde's Rock and you've wowed them.

Everything here seems to have a name already, of course. But if you don't know what they are and want to impress your friends, feel free. Who's to check?

Feel free to use my name, if you want. I wouldn't mind a Thom Rock or a Thom Hill or a Thom Tree.

Why, I wouldn't even mind if you named toilets after me. Why should John be one of the most welcomed names in America?

Ah, nuts, I've strayed from my point, haven't I? I was talking about buying fish for dinner.

So after we walked to Fisherman's Wharf, we watched the monkey for a while and waded on into the usual crowd of six million tourists speaking 732 languages all at the same time.

Did you ever notice how the tourists at Fisherman's Wharf act like they can really see something besides all the other people they're bumping into? Is that wonderment?

They don't smile as much as the people walking along the ocean.

And they do have sea lions barking and begging for food. They have pelicans sitting on rails and eating out of people hands. And they have views of one of the prettiest harbors in the world.

But they still have to tell each other to smile when they point a camera.

Or, as some of the trendy ones do today, they tell each other to do something when they point the video recorder. "Come on, wave or something," seems to be the yuppie version of "say cheese."

But I've strayed from the point again. We wanted fish.

Now mind you, T-shirts and metal ashtrays and brass-plated seashells with thermometers in them seem much more plentiful than fish on the wharf. There are even two — TWO — carmelcorn stands.

There are three — THREE — fish stands on the wharf. But they seem to have plenty of fresh fish lying around, looking up at you from mounds of melting ice.

At least there's enough fish there for dinner. And poking around the fish stands is really kind of interesting, if you can get used to all those eyes looking back at you.

There's the Peninsula Fish Market, which is the cleanest-looking one on Fisherman's Wharf. It has a tile floor, for instance, and shiny faucets. There's a tray of salmon smoking right at the front of the stand, along with warm bagels. There's a delicatessen case with pickled octopus and stuff like that in it. There's also sea-lion food — trays of sardines and mackerel parts for 50 cents each — sitting beside the fresh bass and squid and swordfish.

Across the boardwalk is the Liberty Fish Market. It's smaller, but it has fresh salmon and eel and lots of fish on ice and a tankful of live lobsters for $8.50 a pound.

But we liked Cavaliere's Fish Market, which seemed to have a good variety of fresh fish and a concrete floor that was wet from the melting ice. There were mounds of eyes looking up at us, of course, but there were also steaks from the big fish like tuna, salmon and sword. The squid was $1 a pound — 10 pounds for $9 — and the clerks were willing to wrap it in fresh newspaper.

Hot damn! All we had to do was get it back to the grill.

And clean it, of course. Which is what company is for.

Oh, come on. They got a kick out of it.

And I got a damned good dinner, one of the best I've had on the Peninsula. And it was cheap, too. Except for the wine, dinner for four cost about $25 — squid, prawns, tuna and some token vegetables.

The wine was expensive, sure. Next time, maybe we'll invite more company and let them bring it.

Sacramento Revisited

You CAN Go Back
— If You Want To

Maybe the pope didn't kiss the landing strip at the Monterey Peninsula Airport. But I might.

I sure feel like doing something to show my appreciation.

It's not just that I'm starting to feel at home here, although I am. But I've just gathered fresh evidence about the sad condition of life elsewhere.

I had to go away again, see. This time it was a long-stalled trip back to Sacramento to pick up some of the stuff I stored at friends' houses when I moved down here four months ago.

I had a carload of boxes at one house, a couple hundred records at another, a rocking chair and a painting I didn't want my friends to get too attached to.

It's true I had been imposing and not getting my stuff out of their ways as quickly as I should have. But I wasn't anxious to go back to Sacramento and they all understood that.

It didn't make sense to leave a seaside resort and go back to the Central Valley before temperatures there dropped below 100.

And I also wasn't sure what emotions might be waiting for me in my old town and I wasn't particularly anxious to find out. When you move in your middle ages, there are lots of misgivings to carry with you, and questions that don't have answers.

Surprisingly, it was a really good visit to Sacramento. That dry climate is still natural to my body. The friends I got around to seeing are some of the same ones who have visited me here. The old neighbors I never liked that much weren't home. And I got to spend an entire afternoon with my godson, who was getting his vocabulary in shape for his first birthday.

Weekends should have been that good when I lived there.

There were even some pleasant surprises on the first trip back. The little house that had been both a hobby and an anchor for a decade stirred absolutely no emotions. It didn't seem like my home or a part of me, like I thought it would. It was just a house that I sold to somebody else.

It looked the same, except the tree I planted in the front yard has grown a bit.

I noticed that as I drove by it several times.

I also noticed that the old neighborhood is even prettier than I remembered.

There were some unpleasant surprises too. One of my favorite bars had changed.

It's the one I use as a standard in life, for what bars should be like. It's the one I've been trying to duplicate on the Peninsula.

It's in a seedy section near the state Capitol and has long attracted the most diverse crowd in the world — bag ladies and state officials, hookers and cops, hippies and punks, taxi drivers and newspaper writers, young and old, black and white and red and yellow and brown — because it has reasonable prices, real turkey sandwiches and the best blues band in town playing seven nights a week. Funky stuff that could make you dance or cry, sometimes at the same time.

But since I left, the place has gone Cajun. The band is good all right, but a little bit of Cajun music goes a whole long way. And the crowd has changed. The hippies and punks and old people have been replaced by the colorless yuppies who have pre-packaged hair and labels all over their clothes.

I met some of my old drinking buddies there this weekend. It was a shorter night than we planned.

Partly it was the new music. Partly it was a sort of disinterest in my old life. And partly it was because I noticied that some of my friends have coping problems.

I never realized it when I was around them daily, when I thought their maladjustments and bizarre situations were just some of the foibles of life that are worth talking about.

But with a little distance, the patterns and repetitions are obvious. I think I'm sorry that I noticed that.

But that really has little to do with why I want to kiss the landing strip at the Monterey airport.

I stopped in San Jose while I was on my way to pick up my stuff.

There were some old friends gathered there, people who worked together on the East Coast 15 to 20 years ago, in those formative years when we'd sleep on each others' floors and sofas as often as not.

We're scattered all around these days, doing all sorts of things in the name of journalism. One of us lives in San Jose, obviously. And one of us lives in Washington, D.C., and was here visiting.

We get together once in a while for the reasons old friends always get together — it's comfortable.

I think I've always known that. But it has become clearer because I live in a new town, among people I don't know so well.

Now don't get me wrong. I'm not complaining, just observing.

I've met a lot of people on the Peninsula, most of whom seem very nice and pleasant. There's also something refreshing I've noticed about Peninsula people — they seem genuinely happy to be here. They seem to truly appreciate the unique beauty of this place and they seem delighted to be able to live in it.

That's so pleasant. And infectious.

But even though I've met a lot of folks here who seem likable — and who share my awe with the natural surroundings — new people take time to sort out. As long as human beings are basically afraid of rejection, we have to scout each other at least a little. We're all on trial when we meet. And it's not particularly comfortable.

With old friends, there's no need to parade for each other. Nobody's on trial anymore. They long ago decided to accept your aberrations and you decided to accept their flaws as character traits. You can be comfortable with each other and just enjoy the company without worrying about impressions. You're free to be yourself.

So we got together in San Jose. And that was terrific.

But we also had to *put up* with San Jose. which is what makes me want to kiss the ground here.

San Jose traffic is fast, thick and without turn signals. The freeways are just canyons through tract houses. The smog is heavy. And you can feel the anxiety in people.

When I woke up in the morning I found that my car had been splattered with eggs that somebody tossed in the night.

I decided you've got to expect that sort of thing when you leave the Peninsula, even for a weekend.

So without a lot of fuss, I drove to the nearest car wash.

They got most of the eggs off the finish. But their machines tore off a strip of molding on the side of the car.

The attendants found it and give it back to me. I said, "Thanks." After all, it was only a little bent.

140

In Paradise, You
Need Fewer Trinkets

So it takes four months to unpack here. What's the hurry?

There are tides to watch. And otters. Sunsets. Movements in the fog. And most recently, those fantastic sky shows that materialize when things like storm clouds move across the bay.

Some days here are just gifts.

There are also the fishing boats that probably couldn't make it in and out of the harbor without my eyes fixed on them.

The blue that fills that bowl at the bottom of the hills here also needs a lot of study. It goes from deep sapphire to gunstock gray and if I watch

141

30 or 40 more years, I might figure out why. It's a worthwhile project.

But eventually you have to shirk your obligations to nature and deal with the stuff you shoved in closets and under the bed and off in corners while you were moving in.

You need to finish unpacking.

And sorting.

And tossing out more of the things you should never have moved in the first place.

I think it was the cookbooks that prompted me to action this time.

I've cooked maybe 20 real meals in my life, but I had accumulated a large — and heavy — box of cookbooks over the years.

I don't know why, but I obviously packed them up before I left Sacramento and dropped them at a friend's house to store with a bunch of other stuff. That's the load that I just got around to hauling down to the Peninsula . . . and stacking inside the front door of my new apartment.

When I started to look inside the boxes to see what precious possessions I hadn't missed for four months, it was the cookbooks that seemed to jump up at me.

The long and short of it is that I no longer have them.

Nor do I have an assortment of salt and pepper shakers I never used, funny looking planters from a variety of Christmases and birthdays, a collection of beer and soda cans that used to sit in my kitchen windows and just a whole heap of country-and-western records.

I took a carload to a cousin's garage sale in Santa Cruz and picked up an entire $30 for some of those treasures. I took another carload to the Salvation Army and put at least that much more out on the curb with the garbage.

Sure that stuff should never have been packed and moved. It shouldn't have been collected. But it seems to be some law of nature that we must accumulate enough to fill all the space we have, then start piling. We seem to just pack it without much thought when we move.

Then too, things change. The trinkets I might not have been willing to part with four months ago would just be in the way now. I'm finding that I don't need a lot of my old stuff in paradise.

And at the price of floor space on the Peninsula, I've decided that if you can't wear it, eat it or sleep on it, you probably can do without it.

I've also decided that the real reason we move from time to time is just to shake up our senses and sort out our trinkets.

Obviously, if we didn't want changes we wouldn't move. Which is not to say there aren't going to be second thoughts and questions to haunt us.

It's not a pre-occupation in my new Peninsula setting, but I am finding that I do have some glum moments when I'm pretty sorry and sad. It's part of the normal adjustment process, I think.

The rush from simply moving here is settling down and allowing some flighty emotions. One minute I'm whistling and smiling, the next I'm hurting and trying to hide.

It all seems quite natural and I'm sure it will pass into another phase soon. Why, just the other night I had to pull my car off Holman Highway so I could get out and kick up my heels and shout, "Yiipppeeee!!"

I really did that.

I was just overwhelmed by the thought that I was on Carmel Hill and, damn it, I was almost home. There's still something surreal about just being here.

But I'm also finding that moving is harder than it was 10 years ago. I didn't see so many uncertainties then, when I moved from New York to California. I just wanted to get out of the snow.

But now I'm aware of some of the comfort I've left behind. I think maybe I'm remembering some things as better than they actually were. That probably has to do with age. It gets harder to move on.

Of course, some of the misgivings are tempered by new opportunities. In a lot of ways, moving gives you a chance to start over, a good chance to decide what you want to keep and what you want to throw away.

But those are rarely simple decisions, particularly when you're dealing with emotions and habits and lifestyle.

Maybe that's why we move so many trinkets, so we'll have something symbolic to work with. I did notice the first things I threw out here were spare lamp shades and gifts from old girlfriends.

I think it's really a simplification process. I keep getting rid of stuff here.

In the sorting prompted by the unused cookbooks, I got rid of six boxes of clothes I should never have moved down from Sacramento. Actually, some of them should never have been moved from New York.

It was easier to dump them, of course, after I found out that bell-bottom pants are out of fashion.

I honestly didn't know that. I've never paid much attention to fashion and things like that. Hell, before I moved here I didn't even care about sandcastles.

I've always let my weight fluctuate so dramatically that I've been more worried about what fits than what's in style. Or what comes closest to fitting.

I was a little surprised to find out that bells have been out for several years now. I had several pairs of them in the closet, in several different sizes.

I had a bunch of wide neckties, too. And jackets with narrow lapels. And aging clothes that were four sizes smaller than my present body.

Needless to say, I cleaned out the closet and made another run to the Salvation Army.

At the Sally Thrift Store on Fremont Boulevard, there was a talkative old guy in the collection truck. He was wearing a red baseball cap without an emblem, a brown-and-white plaid shirt, yellow-and black checkered pants and black tennis shoes. He looked a little like Rodney Dangerfield on a golf course.

And yes, he said, he knew bell bottoms were out of fashion.

He took them anyway and asked if any were made from wool.

I didn't know. But I wondered if he had any use for some fancy liquor bottles. Or a papier-mache mushroom with birds painted all over it.

Pretty · Quaint · Home · Towny · Nice

PG is PACIFIC GROVE

CITY OF PACIFIC GROVE CALIFORNIA · INC. 1889

The Fridge Might Hum, But Life's a Ball

I should have known when the handyman I was waiting for waved at me, then walked into the house next door.

I should have at least suspected things weren't going to work out just right.

It's true that my house and the one next door are similar in that they both have three-digit numbers for addresses.

But the handyman had been to my place before.

Twice.

To work on the same refrigerator that still wasn't fixed.

145

And as it turned out, he was there several times more. But all he seemed to do was stand around and look at the malfunctioning refrigerator and tell me he couldn't figure it out.

When it ices up like that, unplug it and let it defrost, he said. Then we'll see what happens.

Hell, I knew that much.

But I was getting annoyed at finding stuff rotting inside a noisy refrigerator that was running around the clock. I didn't mind the milk and cottage cheese so much, but the mayonnaise was getting expensive.

The landlord had picked the handyman and was paying his bill, so I felt obliged to put up with him.

I was, though, almost delighted when I called yet again and the handyman said he couldn't help me because he was having personal problems. If I couldn't wait a week or so, I'd just have to call somebody else, he said.

I called somebody else. He was there the next morning and spent about an hour replacing two small parts. The refrigerator has worked fine since. It's even quieter.

And except for those encounters with the unhandy handyman, I have found living in Pacific Grove the past five months to be almost silky smooth.

Other repair people have come out and fixed things on the first try. Deliveries have been prompt.

And when I've had to leave my apartment for things, I've found that Pacific Grove is probably the most convenient place I've ever lived. The town is so compact that almost everything you need is right nearby.

The Grove Market is just five blocks away, as is the Pacific Grove Floral Co. and Pacific Grove Hardware. There's a good bicycle shop right there, too, a shoe shop and a stationery store.

The bank is four blocks from my apartment, as is a drug store with good birthday cards.

There's a handy department store, Ford's. I like Ford's because it's got a lot of stuff and it's never been crowded. You can get in and out quickly, a fact that probably pleases me more than the store's owners.

There are also a number of OK places to eat in Pacific Grove, but a good bar is hard to find in the town that started out as a tent city for Methodists.

Fortunately I'm only a mile from Cannery Row. It's just all part of the convenience that makes Pacific Grove so livable, I figure.

In a lot of ways, the town is like a city neighborhood. But it's prettier. And more of its stores give away calendars at this time of year.

Now let me stop right here and say I'm not intending to slight any other towns or suggest they might be second-rate to Pacific Grove. I'm just trying to say that I have found Pacific Grove to be a handy place to live on the Peninsula. I know Carmel's nice. And Monterey and Salinas and lots of other places too.

I also don't want to pretend that this "first impression" is any sort of an authoritative, incisive look at Pacific Grove. This is just a Valentine.

I've found the place to be convenient, charming, calm, pretty and just plain nice. And I don't mind saying so. Of course, it doesn't hurt to have a front yard named Monterey Bay.

I live in that funky part crowded down by the water, close to downtown. The fragile Victorians are mixed in with glorified shacks, classic mansions and ticky-tacky apartment houses, all jammed in side by side. It's an eye-catching variety and probably healthy.

I know Pacific Grove has a reputation as a home for old fuddy-duddies. But I haven't found it to be exactly that way. I've met some young, relatively hip people in town, a number of whom seem to work in the bars and restaurants around the Peninsula and live in the small apartments.

There also seems to be an inordinate number of pretty women in the town. And a lot of athletic-looking men.

There are also families, of course, with kids selling today's equivalent of candy and magazines at almost every doorway.

The downtown part is utterly charming. Or quaint, as some people call it.

Actually, cute might be the better word.

The store buildings along Lighthouse Avenue are definitely cute, and they have a timeless grace about them that seems both simple and elegant.

Some of the old Victorian houses have been converted to businesses, some haven't. It's a nice mix.

Even traffic is graceful, moving slowly and carefully without stop-lights or stop signs. Pedestrians step freely into the many crosswalks and cars keep backing out of the diagonal parking places at the sides and in the middle of the main street. That traffic pattern depends on courtesy. And that's nice.

I don't think I've quite figured out how small the town really is, or the whole Peninsula, for that matter. I know I run into the same people as I go about my various errands.

It only took a week to start recognizing faces here. Now I'm having trouble going anywhere without running into somebody I know.

On the last trip to the bank I ran into a political candidate to chat with, a city council member and, naturally, a banker that I had written about.

At the grocery store that day, I ran into a neighbor, the wife of a guy I work with, the daughter of a friend and a fellow who sat at the next table in a restaurant the night before.

I took a walk along the ocean and ran into an innkeeper I know, just sitting there counting the waves.

That was a lot of people for one day and it made everything seem pretty home-towny. I think I liked it.

And the one time I flew out of Monterey Peninsula Airport I allowed myself 30 minutes to get there, 15 minutes to park the car and 30 minutes to check in and get through security. Needless to say, I ended up at the airport with an hour to kill, an hour when I could have been home sleeping.

Or listening to the refrigerator.

Just a Gigolo

Considering
a New Career

I've started house-hunting and I've seen enough already to know this is going to be more pathetic than trying to find something decent to rent.

So far I've come to two truths:

• The houses I like, I can't afford to buy.

• The houses I can afford, I don't like.

This could get really painful.

You probably don't remember, but five months ago, when I moved to the Monterey Peninsula from Sacramento, I was humiliated looking for a place to live. I spent more time than I wanted to sorting through a bunch of junk called rental housing. It was generally overpriced, undersized and dull stuff in noisy neighborhoods.

I looked at more than 30 places before I found an apartment I would live in. And I really felt lucky to have found it, even though it takes about half my paycheck for rent.

Well, I'm thinking now that might have been the easy side of house-hunting, and the bargain.

I've looked at houses you're not safe to undress in that are priced at $120,000.

Honestly, I've been in a couple of places here that seem to be held up only by memories, but the people trying to sell them don't flinch a bit when they explain the foundation work that's needed, the sagging floors, the warped walls, the rotted windows, the charred wiring, the clogged plumbing and the missing roofs.

Sometimes I think half the used-car salesmen in New Jersey have been reborn as real estate dealers on the Peninsula.

Granted, I've been looking at the lower end of house prices here. I mean, I would love one of those Pebble Beach estates big enough for horses to get lost on. But I don't think anybody would trust my credit cards and postdated checks for one.

So I'm in the market where it's considered a plus if the doorknob doesn't fall off in your hand.

Why, one house I looked at in Pacific Grove was priced at $160,000 when I walked in, $135,000 when I walked out. All I did was ask whether it was legal to convert the garage to a second bedroom.

That's the market I have to shop in.

When I went to a series of open houses on Sunday afternoon, I kept running into people I know who were looking at the same houses as possible rentals. They rejected them, too, and all they planned to do was put signs in the windows and wait for the rent checks to roll in.

It's true that I have some tastes that are going to make it tougher to find a house I can afford to buy.

I have virtually decided that I want to live in Pacific Grove, no further than, say, four blocks from the bay.

My thinking on this isn't complicated. I'm still consumed by the beauty of this bay and I want to live near it.

Well, that confines me to the Peninsula and eliminates the places without views or handy access — Marina, Seaside, Sand City, Del Rey Oaks, Carmel Valley and most of suburban Carmel.

Prices eliminate Pebble Beach.

The bayfront in Monterey is too commercial and crowded to want to live on.

The real Carmel is too congested for me.

So that leaves Pacific Grove, which I've already found to be pretty easy to live in anyway.

The only real questions I have now are whether I can afford to buy in Pacific Grove, how much time it might take to find something I like and can afford, how painful the search might be and how much junk I'm going to have to look at along the way.

Now I think there might be one way to avoid all this agony.

But it would require me to abuse this newcomer column in one of the trashiest ways known to journalism. So here goes:

I'm told over and over that there are more women than men on this Peninsula. Indeed, the kind of mail I've been getting at the office illustrates that.

More than a dozen women I've never met before have asked me out, after I've made it clear that I'm fat, about half broke-down and struggling to pay my bills.

Now you're right, that may tell us something about those women.

But it's the number the confounds me. If more than a dozen are willing to ask me out on the basis of something they've read in these "First Impressions," there must be a lot more women out there looking for men.

And some of them are bound to be rich.

Yeah, that's right, we're talking about something despicable here.

But, damn it, this may be the only chance in my life to be gigolo.

And I think I might be willing to do that.

After all, what has working hard for 20 years got me? Seventy pounds of extra weight, ulcers, high blood pressure, a string of marginal romances, heavy boxes of newspaper clippings that are turning yellow in the closet, memories I can barely turn into charming conversations, a car that needs new tires, a pension account that will pay me $368 a month if I live long enough to retire and a bunch of friends that don't have savings accounts either.

So if the right woman gets in touch — yes, translate "right" to "rich" — I think I'm ready for a new career.

In exchange for a house I'd like to live in, I think I could make her a very happy woman.

Hell, if she's rich enough, we could hire the finest doctors to help straighten out this sagging body of mine.

She'd never regret it.

151

Besides, it's probably tax deductible to keep me out of cheap housing. If it's not, I know a number of lawmakers who could fix that oversight if, of course, they are properly entertained in our love nest along the bay.

Think about it ladies . . . uh, *rich* ladies.

No $160,000 fixers-uppers for us. No ma'am. Why, there's a $400,000 Victorian in Pacific Grove that's got our name on it. Or maybe that $600,000 colonial on the water would suit us better.

Of course, If you prefer a Pebble Beach estate, I suppose we could make an offer.

You think about it, while I run to K Mart and get some candles for our first dinner.

KING
NEPTUNE'S
MAGIC

Gazing at Moonlight On the Bay

I know it's a silly game, to try to figure out the most beautiful single sight on the Monterey Peninsula.

But I can't keep from doing it.

Maybe it's the kind of thing that prevents sensory overload.

Maybe it's the kind of thing we have to do in order to write sensible notes on our Christmas cards.

Maybe it's just another way of keeping score in life.

But I keep rating what I'm looking at here, even though my standards are getting higher and higher.

Just when I'm convinced nothing could be prettier, something is.

I've looked at the Lone Cypress under a full moon and thought there has never been a more beautiful sight in the world. This one, bush-like tree, standing out there on a jagged rock with whitecaps licking around it, a silvery ocean behind it, the pale outline of Big Sur or whatever that is in the distance. It's a sight that honeymoons are built around.

But then I watched a sunset from Asilomar and thought, wow, this is it! It was one of those soft fires on the horizon, with bursts of oranges and reds and layers of flat clouds forming bands of charcoal and purples. In front of the flames, the ocean was rolling in ever so gently, just sweeping the glassy beach. Great poems were inspired by that sunset, I'm sure. And maybe some pregnancies.

I was looking for another like it when I saw, yes, something even more stunning.

I saw a full moon rising over Monterey Bay and I really don't think that can be topped. I think that's the most beautiful single sight I've seen on the Peninsula.

I saw the moon as full as a button on a blazer just glide over the hills behind Fort Ord. There was a cloud or two drifting in front, weaving a magical lace for extra romance. The moon changed from orange to silver to white as it slipped into heaven.

The light streamed across the water in narrow bands at first, then it spread across the whole bay so you could see the swell rolling as gently as gelatin. The waves turned to white foam as they splashed against the shore.

I guess I'm going on about this. But it was an inspirational sight, the most beautiful one I've seen here.

Oh, I guess I already said that.

Well, I was near Point Pinos, so I couldn't see the boats and masts in the harbor. I'm sure that would have been a gorgeous foreground.

I couldn't see any buildings either. Or trees.

I could just see water and moonlight.

There was no wind to bite at your face.

And the surf was roaring against the points and rocks, helping block out the rest of the world while reminding you that you were near something very powerful and alive.

I just watched and thought about nothing. And everything.

The scene was as refreshing as it was inspiring.

Later that night I went down to the water near my apartment to lean against a rail at Lovers Point. I've been there before, just to look at the water and the waves and the rocks and sometimes the moonlight.

I've been overwhelmed by that view. And that's where I've been most active at this silly game of trying to rate beauty.

I can't help it.

I'm clearly taken by the water here. That could be a result of growing up in the landlocked Midwest or a throwback to some happy summers I spent on an island in the Atlantic Ocean or just a reaction to living in California's parched Central Valley for a decade.

Or it could be just a matter of good taste.

I know a lot of people who have lived here longer than my five months are drawn to Carmel Valley and other places away from the ocean fog.

But I find even the fog fascinating. I watch it drift by and look for shapes in it, just like you do with clouds on lazy days.

When the fog's not around and the sunshine is, that emerald-blue color in the bay just sparkles and gleams. It makes me burst with pleasure.

Yes, I'm still spellbound after all these weeks.

I've stood at the end of my street when the sun was out and wondered if I was looking at the most beautiful place I've ever been.

That strip of coast between Lovers Point and Hopkins Marine Station is just magic.

I've looked at the way the water carves and shapes the shore. I've looked at the swell rolling in from the horizon like there's something tumbling right underneath the surface. I've watched the big waves that charge right towards you but somehow always stop short and splatter back into the bowl.

I've compared the view to places like Lake Tahoe, the Grand Canyon, Vermont in autumn and the Bavarian Alps, world-class beauty like that.

I can look at it through the front window here. Or I can go down and lean against the rail, sit on a bench, walk along for hours and stay totally mesmerized.

The beauty along the bay, in fact, has added to my weight problem. I find it impossible to walk quickly or ride my bike for any distance without stopping to look at something pretty. That's really crimping the aerobic exercise program that was designed to compensate for sitting at a keyboard too many hours a week.

But the place is just so damned pretty, I don't want to miss it.

And in the moonlight, the bay is utterly exquisite.

I swear, I'm ready to fall in love every time the moon lights the bay. Certainly there's plenty of privacy. I've walked a mile in the moonlight along the oceanside recreation trail and run into only one other person.

It's bizarre. A trail that can be so jammed up at times is so empty at others. But when it's empty and all mine, it makes me feel like the richest person in the world, like I own the place and can keep it all to myself.

I've found the same thing along the 17-Mile Drive, strangely enough. I've taken that drive in moonlight and met only one other car between Pacific Grove and Carmel. It was like I owned the Pebble Beach beaches and could park on any one of them and watch the surf roll in.

It was very romantic.

With a date along, the drive could have been worth the $5 toll.

But on the night I discovered the full moon rising, I also discovered that there are a number of lovers' lanes in Pacific Grove I had never noticed before.

In the no-toll mile between Point Pinos and Lovers Point there are several of those very small turnouts and driveways that are just big enough for a car or two.

They were all taken that night. There was at least one couple cuddled in every place I found.

But I may try to beat everybody to one of those places on the next full moon, if I can find the right rich widow to take along.

156

Nature's Art Museum

"Sea at the Point"

A Solution For
After-Holiday Blues

I'm not sure if people who live in a place like this get the after-holiday blues like people who live everywhere else.

But if we do . . . I've found a solution.

Take $3 and go down to Point Lobos for a few hours. If that doesn't perk you up, you'd better start thinking of a place to scatter your ashes.

I just made my first trip down there and I was surprised to find out how close it is (just a couple of miles south of Carmel), how uncrowded it is at this time of year (park in any lot) and how varied the beauty is (trees, rocks, ocean and sea lions).

I had started down once before, right after Thanksgiving, when there were 76 million tourists and 465,327 recreational vehicles on Highway 1, all telling me to go home where I belong.

I stayed in and watched rented movies the rest of that weekend. See how quickly we learn to share? Simply by avoiding.

But on an OUT OF SEASON weekend, hell, it was like driving to the dry cleaners.

I needed to check out Point Lobos because the regional director of the state Parks and Recreation Department calls the reserve "the crown jewel" in the state park system.

Now that takes some imagination because I know a number of other state parks that are unbeatable.

Patrick's Point, in the redwood forest above Eureka, has always been my favorite. There's something spiritual there for me. I can walk along the old Indian trails and sit for hours at abandoned Yurok village sites. I've vacationed there regularly, looking at redwoods and wildflowers and just getting away from telephones for a while.

Then there's the sugar pine forest at Lake Tahoe. It's like a Disney fantasy, with majestic trees so gigantic they cast off pine cones as big as a bucket. About 20 will fill the trunk of a car, the good ones for decorations, the smashed ones for kindling.

Frankly, I thought Point Lobos might need a little goose to get up to that caliber of company. So I figured I'd look for passing whales while I was there. I hear it's that time of year.

But you know, I'm not sure if I saw any whales or not. And it really didn't matter because I was so busy looking at other stuff that's in the park.

I saw a grove of Monterey cypress trees, all bent and compressed by the winds. I think I especially like their twisted trunks. There's history and survival in those gnarls.

I saw a herd of sea lions, all bunched up on rocks too high for the surf. Most of them were sleeping in the sun. Some of them were barking.

I saw the sun backlighting the water, making the ripples look like lumps on a mirror.

And I saw the varied rock of the headlands, cut and piled by waves that never stop beating against it.

I also watched some of the big rocks move. I haven't figured this out exactly, but I know that if you watch the rocks in the surf long enough, you can see them move against the water. They appear to move into the waves, then drift in the opposite direction of the flow.

I think this needs more study.

So does the effect of lighting at Point Lobos.

Why, the whole coastal scene changes when you shift your position and change the angle of sunshine.

From one side, the rocks along a cove appeared to be covered with moss, black and sparkling in the sun. But from the other side, they looked like common brown rocks, bare and dry.

It's one of those magic games nature plays.

And a couple of hours of games like that sure breaks up what too quickly becomes routine. A day trip to Point Lobos is like a mini-vacation.

The place is beautiful, yes, and possibly a crown jewel.

But more importantly to me, I think, is that it opened up my head like I hadn't expected it to do. I guess I didn't realize how badly I needed to just get away for a few hours.

Before I moved here, I often vacationed on the Monterey Peninsula because this is such a peaceful place.

When I needed to just stop for a while, I could come down and sit on the beach at Carmel or walk along Lovers Point or hang out at Fisherman's Wharf, fill my lungs with fresh air, my eyes with beauty and just let my mind ramble wherever it needed to go.

I'd avoid people for a couple of days and just brood when I needed to, letting ideas take shape and letting decisions make themselves.

I've made marriage decisions while vacationing here. Job decisions, too. I've outlined books that never got written. Conceived of potential Pulitzer Prize-winning stories.

I've also spent plenty of time with the mundane, deciding what kind of tires to buy for my car and things like that.

But now that I live here, I can't run off to the Peninsula anymore just to think. You can't vacation in vacationland when you live here.

There's always work to do. Or somebody visiting. Or calls that need to be made, letters that need answers. There's usually laundry waiting. And dishes in the sink, shower stalls that need scrubbing, rugs that need vacuuming.

You actually need a vacation from vacationland once in a while. Just a little escape to freshen your mind.

I think I got to Point Lobos just in time.

Indeed, one minute I was focusing the binoculars so I could scan the horizon for whales. But the next I was thinking through a letter that had made me mad the day before.

I snapped back and noticed how the water line on the rocks told that the tide was going out. Then I drifted again, this time to things that normally rest deep in my soul. I remembered a poem someone sent me years ago, about fresh starts and new beginnings. And I wondered how she's getting along these days.

I walked a little way through the cypress. Other people came along and I walked away from them.

I wandered over to a cliff, then to another and walked along the ocean for a while, just letting my mind unclog itself and ramble all over my life.

I thought about unimportant things, like whether to buy a new lens for my camera, and profound things, like the nature of love.

I'm not sure I decided anything that day. But then, I'm not sure I needed to. It was just a little getaway.

"That's a whale of a whale!"

Off the Coast —
A Whale of a Show!

If you get close enough, you can hear the "whoooooshhh" of the air they push out.

Then sometimes there's a suction behind that, a rush of air through a tube that makes the raspy "ahhhhhhhh" you get when you blow across the top of a pop bottle.

Those are the sounds whales make when they breathe, and I never heard them before I went for a boat ride on Monterey Bay.

Neither had I seen them jump out of the water like salmon.

Nor had I imagined so many of them in one place — 14 in one

sighting, about a mile from Cypress Point.

Awesome isn't a good enough adjective to describe the whale show that's going on right off shore.

Spellbinding is better.

But I found it exhausting.

A half-hour look there at the three whales that are surfacing in unison, look there at the mother and her calf, look there at the one moving in close, look there at the geyser field on the horizon, look there at that one jumping.

Wow!!!!!

And double WOW!!!!!

I went out twice this month, with Herald photographer Robert Fish on his annual whale-shooting trip and with one of the 15 commercial fishing whale-watching boats that leave Fisherman's Wharf about every hour.

And I'd like to go out again and again.

Even if you don't see any whales, which is possible, you get to look back at a gorgeous panorama — the entire horseshoe of hills around the bay. I didn't realize before how truly narrow is the band of settlements around the water. And I didn't realize how many gaudy-looking buildings sit out on pilings in the bay.

Nor did I realize what a landmark I had picked in a scraggly row of trees on the top of Carmel Hill. I've used those trees to get my bearings on the Peninsula, when I've been totally confused about north-south-east-west because of the curvature here. But that same row of trees stands out from the water, so you can figure roughly where you are and relate points on the shore.

The surf is just as stunning from the other side. And it breaks best at Point Joe, Asilomar State Beach, Point Pinos, Lovers Point and on the rocks at the end of 14th Street in Pacific Grove.

And drifting around in calm water on a sunshiny day is one of the most soothing things you can do.

People without yachts may not know that.

But the commercial fishing boats that take out whale-watchers at this time of year charge only $10 a head for a ride that lasts about two hours. It's one of the best bargains you can find, at least when the sea is gentle and the sun is shining.

It can be a carnival ride on the way out of the bay and on the way back in, as the boat dashes between the swells and occasionally sprays seawater up onto the passengers.

But once past Point Pinos — five or six miles from the wharf, maybe a

162

mile off shore — the boat drifts and lulls the whale-watchers.

There were about 30 of us when I went out on the New Roz, a Monterey Sport Fishing boat that needs some varnish.

We lined up along the sides and talked in a variety of languages — English, Spanish and German were the only ones I recognized — while we scanned the horizon and smiled at each other.

Most of us had cameras and we wanted the whales to surface and pose.

But, of course, the 16,000 gray whales that migrate along the West Coast between feeding and breeding waters rarely show themselves as much as you would like.

They rarely jump up out of the water like small fish do during migrations. Naturalists call such leaps breaching. But Robert Fish, who has photographed several of them, calls it jumping out of the water. They both make sense, but I was with Fish when I saw them — one whale off Spanish Bay that jumped up three times, another that jumped six times — so I'll use his terminology.

I'll even quote his expression. "Lookatthat, lookatthat, lookatthat," he yelled, as he kept his camera on motor drive.

I sort of mumbled an "Oh, wow!" while I stared and marveled.

It is truly humbling to see a 40,000-pound animal, 45-feet long, a swimmer by nature, just pop out of the water, arch as gracefully as a salmon and slide back in.

I really don't think I have the right words to describe it.

It is obviously a thrill.

And the highlight of any whale-watching trip lucky enough to encounter it.

But we saw about 30 other whales that day too, several of them performing in one way or another.

There were so many near Cypress Point that it was like wandering into the middle of a herd.

Most stayed in the distance and we could see only the geyser-like mist they sprayed as they exhaled, then their barnacled brown and gray backs and tails as they dived back into the Pacific.

They seemed as playful as dolphins in marine shows.

The whale show off the commercial fishing boat was only slightly less spectacular. That boat didn't go out as far or stay as long as the photographer's did. But it enountered at least 17 whales on the two-hour treat.

At one point, there was a group of three entertaining us about 100 yards from the boat. They surfaced three of four times in a row, then dived and stayed under the water for five or six minutes before surfacing a half-mile away. "Whooooshhh," float across the surface like a barrel, arch the back, thrust the tail and dive.

On the other side of the boat, there was a mother and a newborn calf, which looked so tiny in comparison, even if it was maybe 10 feet long. When the baby surfaced to breathe beside its mother, it exhaled such a faint mist that you couldn't always see it.

There was another whale performing near the shore.

There were two behind us.

And in the distance, there was a group of four spouting geysers along the horizon.

The water was so alive with whales, it's going to be hard to look out at the ocean again without believing they are still there. If they're out of sight, maybe it's because they're right under the surface, getting ready to jump up.

Suffering
in Paradise

The euphoria lasted four months, maybe five.

Then a little malaise set it.

It wasn't anything awful, just enough to make me feel off-balance and start looking for imperfections in this Peninsula paradise.

I thought it was just the holidays getting to me. Or maybe a virus.

The symptoms were so vague at first that it took a while to recognize that what I had was a simple, old-fashioned, uncomplicated case of homesickness.

That's right, homesick in heaven.

Who would have thought that would happen?

Who would have thought that you could live here, in one of the most beautiful and treasured parts of the world, and think longingly about someplace else?

For that matter, who would have thought you could miss Sacramento?

It's one of the most unexpected problems I've encountered since I moved to the Peninsula six months ago.

At some point, I know I started feeling guilty about moving. But that wasn't because I had moved here. That was because I had moved anywhere, knowing I had left some people behind, close friends whose lives and psyches were tied into mine.

You hurt people when you leave them and I don't think I really knew that before.

You also miss them. But I knew that would happen.

Then too, I've been brooding about some lesser things I left behind — an economy geared to civil servants' incomes, for example. Affordable houses with extra rooms in them. Garages. Driveways. A discount store with clothes in my size. A wine shop where somebody knows what's in the bottles. Free TV. Good bars.

I've also missed the ethnic variety of people I used to work with and hang out with in the capital of the most diverse state in the world. The Peninsula I've been living in is awfully white. European cultures are okay, of course, but they can be stuffy.

And at times, I've felt a little shut out here. I don't know if it's me or the cliquishness on the Peninsula, but there have been times when I've wondered if I belong here.

I was beginning to wonder if moving here might have been a mistake.

It's all part of the adjustment process, I think. But moving seems to be harder as you get older. It seems to be harder on both sides of the packing crates — harder to leave one place, harder to adjust to the next.

Maybe it was just the holidays after all. Or the messages on the Christmas cards.

But when I finally realized I was actually homesick, I cured it with a weekend trip back to the old place.

It was my first real visit, with no business that needed attention, nothing to get out of storage, no special visitors from other towns to see. I went back simply to visit because I missed it.

I surrounded myself for a long weekend with people I love and trust, people who let me uncork myself and just chatter mindlessly late into the nights, as if it were important.

166

There are people who have let me do that here. But it's just not the same when you don't know them so well. They ask questions and sometimes debate, rather than seeing that it's just babble, a way to organize the notes in your head, kind of like writing a newspaper column.

Maybe some day, if I ever leave the Peninsula, they will have become the people I'll be homesick for then.

But for now, I needed to see the people I can't replace.

I needed to have a drink with a particular friend in a Sacramento bar where I've said a lot of hellos and a lot of goodbyes.

I needed to watch my year-old godson walk and dance on his unsteady legs. And I needed to hear his seven-word vocabulary — eight, if you'll accept "num-num" as a word.

I needed to see his mother, who is my closest friend in life, and make sure she and her family are getting along okay without me to mediate their disputes.

I needed to see the friends who took time off from work to move me down here last summer, friends who have listened to my babbling for years. I needed them to see if my spirit has changed.

And I didn't know it until I did it, but I needed to go back to my old newsroom and see somebody else sitting at my desk. Using my computer terminal. Talking on my phone.

Part of moving is a turning-loose process, I guess. There is something like grieving to be done. And that too takes longer than I thought it would.

The long vacation here is over. Life is getting a little rocky again.

Actually, Sacramento turned out to be quite a pleasant place to visit. In the winter, anyway.

The place seems bigger to me now. There are more roads with more lanes to more shopping centers than I noticed before.

And the houses . . . Wow!!! They are so big with so many rooms and so many nooks and crannies . . .

My entire apartment here can fit into a friend's living room there.

I had forgotten that not everybody has to keep the guest bed in the dining room.

And store the brooms behind the kitchen stove.

And keep their files under the bed.

In a way, it was reassuring to see what I left behind. I think I needed to know that there is a world still there, that life goes on without me.

That makes me feel less guilty about moving to Shangri-La.

It also makes me think I can go back and visit the next time I feel homesick. And I'm sure that I will.

Next time, though, I'll recognize the ghosts and second-thoughts and lingering doubts quickly for what they are — homesickness.

I'm pretty sure I don't want to move back there. I mean, I came here looking forward and I'd like to continue that way.

But I think I might need to visit from time to time, like people who return to their childhood homes for Christmas.

I realize I could be the only person in the world that thinks of Sacramento as a resort.

But I did leave chunks of my heart all over that town. And I left pools of blood on a newsroom floor. I spent a lot of my younger self during my 10 years there and several of the six or eight or 10 true friends you're allowed in a lifetime are still there.

Maybe the old cliche doesn't work for all of us. Maybe home isn't just where you hang your hat.

Getting Out, Enjoying Bad Weather

Now I'm confused again.

I've spent a lifetime learning to stay indoors on rainy days.

But when you move to a place like this, maybe the old wisdom isn't good enough anymore.

If you stay in out of the rain here, you miss one of the best shows on the Monterey Peninsula. Storms do wonderful things to this place.

The ocean takes on a whole new life, swirling and whipping mighty waves against the rocks along the shore.

I'd heard of 40-foot waves before, but I'd never seen them until I drove past Pescadero Point in a storm. (For other newcomers: That's along 17-Mile Drive in Pebble Beach, the northern tip of Carmel Bay, a point marked by a "Ghost Tree" sign.)

A giant swell was crashing against the big rocks that stand along Pescadero Point, throwing waves that must have been at least 40 feet high flying into the air with a roar.

The handful of people who put up with the bone-chilling rain to stand and watch that spectacular show giggled, took pictures and applauded.

I hadn't expected to be one of them, but I may be a regular from now on.

I can't imagine why so few people told me about the beauty of storms before.

Oh, I knew, of course, that the waves churned up in the winds. I've seen that from my apartment window. Lovers Point frequently has waves 15 to 20 feet high.

But I didn't know waves could get quite so spectacular — anywhere — in a less-than-historic storm.

I had to stumble across this delightful information while I was driving to Carmel for lunch.

It happened to be a weekend when I had company from out of town. And when we woke up to see the storm wasn't lifting, I thought we'd just drive along the splashing water, stop for a cozy lunch, then maybe rent some movies and head home to a fireplace.

Now I know to save that indoor stuff for windless, rainless days. You can stay in and watch films when the sun is shining, by damn.

It wasn't just the Pescadero Point surprise. Those were the biggest waves I've ever seen. But the whole day in the storm was fairly stunning.

I'd never noticed before all the moss hanging from the trees in Pebble Beach. I'd also never noticed how many of the trees seem to be growing in tangles from granite rock.

I'd never driven all the way out Carmel's Scenic Drive before. I didn't know about all of those big houses overlooking that bay. I had always thought Carmel was a quaint village of little cottages jammed in against each other. I've even wondered how people who live so closely in such small spaces could be so Republican.

Fortunately, the sociology lesson was short-lived.

The storm kept our eyes on the waves and the sea mostly. We decided to skip lunch so we could shoot down to Point Lobos and see what a storm does to that collage of beauty.

It's rare you find anything quite so exotic.

And *that* is coming from what is increasingly a spoiled, Peninsula perspective.

It was on the cliff above Sea Lion Rocks that the kid in me wakened. We were watching the surf charge into the coves that form the Point Lobos shoreline. The swell was relentless and the mighty waves kept beating against the rocks and headland and washing over them.

The rocks came alive with overflows and backflows and waterfalls prancing everywhere along them. Until the next wave charged in.

The swell filled the horizon — miles in every direction from that cliff. It was churning and rolling and heaving. You could see the biggest waves form a minute or two out, then roll in through that rippling swell and CRASH!

The sky overhead was busy too. Dark clouds rolled across while lighter clouds formed shapes and let beams of light streak through occasionally.

It was absolutely mesmerizing.

And worth every health risk my mother ever warned me about. Pneumonia would have been a fair price for that view.

The rain was biting and the wind was ripping through our clothes, but we stood it long enough to walk the length of the cliff.

When we got back to the car, we turned on the heater and drove along the rutted road of Point Lobos to see even more. The waves were whipping up all along one side of the car. And deer were eating in the meadows on the other side.

Honest to God, a half-dozen deer were standing beside the road munching in the bone-chilling wind and the steady drizzle.

Where could we have rented that movie? What lunch could have been better?

All of a sudden I realized there's no such thing as too much of the Peninsula. And there's nothing about it that you can take for granted. You have to keep looking at it.

A storm makes this place dramatic. Just like sunshine dazzles it and the moonlight softens it. This paradise keeps changing.

The tourist in me was fully alive. Again.

So at dark, we drove into Carmel. We got a cup of gelato and walked along in the rain, window-shopping on a nearly deserted Ocean Avenue.

I guess I hadn't done that for a while because I was surprised to see how many T-shirt shops there are in Carmel these days. There are at least four on the chi-chi shopping street.

There is also a lot of bizarre art for sale.

We got so carried away as tourists that when the rain stopped for a while, we went into Clint's bar for a drink.

Oh, I know. I know.

But my company insisted.

I had described the Hog's Breath Inn as a Hollywood casting call, based on my only visit one summer Saturday night. There were exceptionally pretty women and muscular men jammed into the courtyard that night, all staring at the door to see who was walking in to discover them.

But on a rainy night in winter, the pretty people weren't there. It was just us and the other tourists in an outdoor setting that had lots of empty seats.

We found a bench in front of one of the outdoor fireplaces and sat down to get warm and watch the flames from the gas jets. It was so pleasant that night that we had another round of spiked coffees.

A tourist with an infant in her arms joined us on the bench and asked all the common questions: How big is Carmel? How many tourists are there? How's the mayor mayoring?

Hell, I didn't know. But I knew I was hungry and getting primed for a late-night lunch.

That's when the tour sort of stopped. We went over to one of my favorites, the Rio Grill. Spectacular days should always close with braised duck and wild rice, I believe.

At least, if the wine is right.

Thom's Elusive 'Affordable Housing'

This househunting business is starting to get me down.

I've looked at more than 30 now, enough to know that clean sinks and hidden laundry aren't required for open houses in Monterey County. I've sat with a real estate salesman as he tore apart my finances and abilities and told me the prospects are even bleaker than I imagined.

And I've spent countless hours looking at the multiple-listing book where real estate people advertise the houses they can't sell right away.

And what it all comes down to — the old bottom line, as they say — is that I'm all but priced out of the Peninsula where I work.

I'm starting to feel like one of the domestics let in to scrub, but not allowed to hang around for dinner.

Well, maybe I'm not feeling quite that bad. Yet.

But psychedelic buses on the beach are starting to make a lot of sense to me.

Unless, of course, I can bring the tents back to Pacific Grove.

Or force the settlers to get off the land that may belong to my ancestors.

Okay, okay. But you've got to admit, it might be worth trying.

While I think this through, I just wish people around here would stop talking about "affordable" housing while pointing to quarter-of-a-million-dollar tract houses.

I can't afford that.

And the numbers surfacing here indicate that most Peninsula residents can't afford that. We're becoming a colony of renters.

There should be a rule that says when a house is priced at more than, say $90,000, the word affordable can never be attached to it.

Hey, set the price wherever you want it. Higher or lower. That's the beauty of being arbitrary.

I picked the $90,000 figure because that's about what a Herald reporter's salary will buy in this housing market.

That's what the real estate salesman told me.

Reporters are as good a gauge as any, because they usually make middle-of-the-road salaries — enough to buy reliable automobiles but not enough to vacation in Carmel.

If we take us as a model, we know generally that policemen and letter carriers and most accountants can also afford $90,000 houses. Which means that clerks and servers obviously can't, while corporate bureaucrats and drug dealers can, as always, afford whatever they want.

Oh, feel free to do your own job descriptions. That's arbitrary too.

I have to say here, though, that I can afford more house than the average reporter because I bring with me as a down payment the sum I once mistook as a killing on the house I sold in Sacramento.

That and a paltry amount of money I make by writing on the side could bring my price range to $140,000, the real estate man told me.

Now to my way of thinking that's a considerable amount of money and it made me feel that working 60 hours a week is finally starting to pay off . . . until I looked at the average house price on the Monterey Peninsula.

The multiple-listing book, the one that's printed in amazingly small type, showed me that there wasn't a single house for sale at $140,000 in

Pebble Beach or Carmel Highlands. Houses in both places started at $225,000 and raced right up into the millions.

Scratch Pebble Beach.

There was only one place in Carmel for $140,000 — a 400-square-foot structure that sure sounded like a converted garage. The next cheapest was $165,000, a relatively massive house with 650 square feet.

Good-bye, Carmel.

There was only one in Carmel Valley, too, a two-bedroom house that was only a few blocks from the nearest road. The cheapest house actually on a road was $160,000.

So long, Carmel Valley.

Now in Pacific Grove, that looked like another story. There were eight houses listed in my price range — eight houses under $140,000.

But I knew all eight of them and I knew that three were already sold, even before the listing book was printed. One of the others — at $107,000, the cheapest house for sale in Pacific Grove — didn't have a roof on it and had been exposed to the weather for months. One didn't have a foundation. Two were tiny and looked like converted garages. And the eighth one sat right beside a late-night diner.

Sorry, Pacific Grove.

In Monterey, the Peninsula's core city, there were five houses in my price range. But three of those needed rebuilding, the ads said. And the other two were converted garages.

Keep listing, Monterey.

There seemed to be a bonanza in Seaside. More than half of the 65 houses listed for sale there were under $140,000 — 25 of them under $90,000.

But that has got to make you wonder. There is obviously something wrong if Seaside houses are priced so far below the rest of the Peninsula.

Houses are about half-price there, listed from a low of $55,000 to a high of $175,000. It's probably no surprise that the most expensive house for sale in Seaside is cheaper than the cheapest house in Pebble Beach.

But I haven't lived here long enough to know what that means. I wonder if we're looking at some simple racism. Or if we've got a city ravaged by absentee landlords, frightened by crime or suffering from its proximity to Fort Ord.

There may be some of all of that going on, or something else entirely. I just don't know.

Only one real estate agent I've encountered here mentioned race as a reason for Seaside's lower property values. One mentioned schools. Two mentioned drugs. Two mentioned the Army. I wondered about the limited access to the bayshore.

But I think a half-price city is worth looking at. There have got to be housing bargains there and maybe I can find one.

I thought there might be some good deals in Marina, too, where places listed for $67,500 to $170,000. I decided to go up and check that out. I'll give you a full report later.

But if we can exclude Seaside and Marina from the numbers for a minute, let me tell you that I counted 502 houses listed for sale on the rest of the Peninsula — 75 in Pebble Beach, 40 in Carmel Highlands, 130 in Carmel, 140 in Carmel Valley, 42 in Pacific Grove and 65 in Monterey.

And there were 15 in my price range — the "Thom affordable housing," we might call it.

That's 3 percent of Peninsula houses priced for a middle-of-the-road wage earner who has goosed his buying power about 50 percent.

And those houses are the converted garages, the ones that need rebuilding — or tearing down — and the ones without roads.

Oh, yeah, there was also a commercial lot in Monterey in my price range. An empty, commercial lot. An empty, commercial lot that might make a dandy place to park a psychedelic bus.

Learning About
Real Estate

I almost bought the cutest little house in Pacific Grove.

It was a one-bedroom cottage jammed in with others like it on a narrow street about four blocks from the ocean.

It had 650 square-feet, lots of windows and no yard to speak of.

It was almost perfect for me.

Except it didn't have an ocean view, which I've about realized I can't afford anyway. And it didn't have room for a spare bed, which is becoming less important as I take a closer look at Peninsula prices.

This place was $135,000.

Now if you think about that for a minute, it's a little ridiculous. That's more than $200 a square-foot for a frame house without a view, a garage or a yard.

And I thought it was a good buy.

The young couple who had lived in it, remodeled it and were selling it had done everything just right. They had kept the bathtub with the claw feet while installing a modern, low-flush toilet. They lined the bedroom ceiling with incense cedar, kept the natural wood finishes on the French doors and wainscoting they installed, put in a wood-burning stove instead of one of those icky free-standing fireplaces, arranged the kitchen around a butcher block and built a shed out back for the washer and dryer.

I looked at the place during a Sunday afternoon open house and really felt that I should buy it right on the spot. It's exactly what I can afford and it was ready to live in and it was close enough to what I want. I've looked long enough to know that's a rare combination.

I also liked the people selling it. The woman of the couple, another Illinois native, recognized me from these newcomer columns and said I'm better looking in person than the newspaper drawings indicate.

She's right, of course.

But I would have wanted to buy her house anyway. Flattery may be rare in this world, but I don't think it's worth the price of a house. At least, not if you have to work for the mortgage payments.

Unfortunately, I'm a Virgo. I'm rarely poised for immediate action, like I should have been that day. I decided to go ahead as planned and look at some other houses that were open that afternoon.

It took several hours, a dozen open houses and a phone consultation with some smarter friends in Sacramento to decide that I had found the house I want to live in.

But by then, there were already two other offers on the house. I took number three and got in line, like in a butcher shop.

And I learned something about Peninsula real estate that day. And about myself.

If I see that place again, I will write a check on the spot and unroll my sleeping bag on the living room floor if necessary.

Although I'm sorry it got away, that one was actually the second house I lined up for during the eight months that I've lived here.

The other one was in Pacific Grove too, a slightly bigger cottage that actually looked out over the bay. It sold for less money and I missed out on it because I didn't think of the possibilities.

I noticed that house was for sale while I was out walking one day. But I

178

assumed it was out of my price range, so I didn't even ask about it.

A few months later, I saw some real estate listings that indicated that house was $122,000. I called immediately and found that it had just been sold.

What was wrong that it was selling so far below the market value, I asked.

Well, it was a divorce sale.

The wife, who was living in it, didn't want to sell the house. So she wouldn't let anybody inside to look at it, the husband said.

Trying to sell a house that nobody could see kept the place on the market four months and drove the price down from the original $160,000.

When it hit the $122,000 mark, the wife inexplicably let in some people who knocked on the door and asked to see the place, the husband said.

They bought it that afternoon.

Gee, didn't she understand, I asked, that she was cutting herself out of half the equity and losing thousands of dollars her way?

"Why do you think I'm divorcing her?" was his only answer.

He left me with a haunting feeling that I may meet that woman some day and get involved with her. Lord, have mercy!

On my bad days, I think of her.

On my good days, I think that I've now seen two houses I could buy. There will be a third.

Meanwhile, I've been amusing myself at more open houses than I should have gone to.

I checked out Marina, like I said I would, and found out that it's not for me.

Oh, there are some nice houses there at good prices. I saw a couple that I would consider buying if I had a family to house or if floor space was more important to me. But I don't and it isn't.

I went to eight open houses there one Sunday afternoon and looked at houses under my $140,000 limit that had three bedrooms in them and at least two bathrooms. Three had huge back yards for grass, gardens or kids.

None of the locations was perfect — too close to the noisy freeway, right behind a shopping center, surrounded by apartment houses, in neighborhoods where houses had iron bars on the windows.

But some of them would do if they had to, especially for the price and the size. A dollar seems to buy about twice as much house in Marina as it does on the Peninsula. Plus you get a yard.

179

Most of the Marina I looked at is fairly typical of California tract developments.

One thing I liked a lot was the ethnic diversity I saw there — white kids riding their skateboards with black kids and brown kids and yellow kids. That's the way I think the world is supposed to be and this son of an Indian found it refreshing.

But Marina is not for me. It's too isolated from the ocean. I mean, it's right *on* the ocean, but it's kept back from it by a freeway, an RV park and sand dunes, in that order.

You can hear the ocean in parts of Marina. You can certainly smell it. But you can't see it unless you go down Reservation Road and enter the state park that includes the beach. That's just not what I'm looking for.

Maybe I've become a snob, but I've been trying my damnedest to stay within view of that ocean. I think that's why I moved here in the first place.

In serious house-hunting, I quickly ruled out Salinas and places inland simply because they are too far from the ocean. At least, for now.

Something else bothers me about Marina — I'd have to use the Highway 1 freeway to commute to my job in Monterey. I think that would bother me a great deal, daily.

I'm afraid I'd feel like a capsule, like I really wasn't connected to the Peninsula I've fallen in love with.

I also wouldn't like to drive by an Army shooting range twice a day.

Like I say, it would be more interesting if I had different values — like a family and kids.

But in my lifestyle, I see extra bathrooms as more things to clean.

And I see yards as work that I don't care to do.

The Peninsula may not want me — it may have priced people like me out of this economy. But I think I'll keep looking, just in case.

Pacific Grove Gothic

Reporter Joins
Ranks of Homeowners

Ho ho ho ho ho!
I found a house.
Ha ha ha ha ha!
It's the little one I wanted.
Hee hee hee hee hee!
The deal's in escrow.
 And now I just want to sit back and feel smug for a while.
 And gloat.
 If nothing else, this means my Sunday afternoons are free.

No more house hunting, at least for a while.

No more digging through *The Herald*'s classifieds to find the house ads that say "cute," "cozy," "starter," "investment property" or other such code words for small and comparatively cheap.

No more wondering about this city or that one, this neighborhood or the street.

No more open houses to see if there's a roof above and a foundation below.

No more looking at other people's rutted yards and worn carpets and dirty sinks.

No more measuring to see if my desk would stick out and block the doorway.

And no more talking to strangers about my paltry savings account and my working person's cash flow — either in weekly, monthly or annual terms.

The deal's been done.

And a lot of the decisions I haven't made yet will now be made for me.

Among other things. I don't have to worry if I belong on the Peninsula anymore. Or if I really want to stay around for a while.

Hell, I've got weeds to cut now and sidewalks to sweep and taxes to pay. Commitments and responsibilities. When would I have time for any more soul-searching?

Even if I'm not sure that home-owning is a whole lot of fun, I know I feel relieved just to have found a house that I could afford here. It's a bonus that I actually like it.

It's not a very big house and you can't see the ocean through the windows and it doesn't have a fireplace.

But it's really pretty spiffy anyway. And it's certainly cute. And cozy. And I think I'm going to like it a lot.

It's also all I can afford.

I looked at more than 30 alleged houses in the $140,000 range, looking at converted garages, shoeboxes with rotting floors and houses that need moats filled with alligators around them to be reasonably safe.

The one I found has only one bedroom in a total of 650 square feet. But it's been thoroughly rebuilt by a young couple so proud of their work they took progress photos every few weeks.

It's also in Pacific Grove, where I've really fallen for the village atmosphere.

It sits on only a half-lot on a narrow street that has a lot of other little houses on it. They're mostly board-and-batten houses, that construction style that looks something like orange crates with roofs. Some of them were built right around the tents of the 19th century settlers. Mine wasn't, but it's about that same size and shape.

Of course it's not the oceanfront dream I had when I moved here eight months ago. But that turned out to cost $400,000.

It's not one of the huge Victorians everybody likes. Those are about $300,000.

It's not even the two-bedroom house I left behind in Sacramento. That would be about $200,000 here.

But it is damned cute and it has a driveway and porches in front and back.

There's such a market for houses in this price range in this condition that it took Linda Michaels and Greg Frederick about two hours to sell it.

I got it through the third offer of the day, a backup offer I had no faith in. The first offer was withdrawn in about a week by folks who had second thoughts about the financing. The second was turned down because it was from a lawyer and the sellers don't like lawyers. Then there I was, an honest reporter with a check in one hand, a suitcase in the other.

We talked a little bit about the actual price, who would pay what fees and charges in the transaction, when we would move and other stuff like that. It was pretty easy and agreeable.

Until they hired a real estate man to draw up a formal contract. Then we had some problems.

He wanted to specify where I could borrow money for the house, a demand that rubbed me wrong and threatened to cost me extra money in loan fees. He said he was afraid that a lender not familiar with Peninsula prices would buckle at the last minute and not see the $135,000 value of a tiny house on half a building lot.

We talked it through and struck a new deal that cost us all a few more bucks. I was trying not to let this house go, regardless of the new costs. And they were trying to avoid the selling ordeal again, regardless of how marketable the house is.

So I applied for a mortgage where they wanted and put the deal in escrow.

While we're waiting for the money people to do whatever it is money people do, I've started sorting through the closets. Again. And trying to figure out what to dump first.

It is a very small house.

And I feel very lucky to have found it.

More than lucky, actually. I feel like I've accomplished something in this housing market.

It certainly takes the pressure off trying to be a gigolo for a rich widow. Or becoming city manager of Monterey. Or winning the lottery.

Still, the bank says I can barely afford the house payments, even though they will be less than the rent I've been paying. I guess that's not a surprise.

I'm getting one of those funny-money mortgages that I wouldn't have even considered before I got a cold dose of Peninsula prices. It's a variable interest rate that starts with low payments and jumps up in stages. You can defer the higher payments if you want and stretch a 30-year loan to 40 years or 50 years.

It all sounds pretty squirrelly, but it's the only thing that seems to work here for my income bracket.

I went to eight different mortage companies before we agreed on a particular one. And I found the same basic story. I also found there are a lot of variables and differences from one company to the next.

I always thought mortgage companies were like gasoline stations — their prices are equally high so you go to the one that's most convenient.

But that's not the case at all. Pushed into a mortgage search by a businesswoman who knew what she was doing, I found different possibilities at every bank I checked. The up-front loan fees ranged from zero to $2,400, the monthly payments from $750 to $1,200.

There were dozens of small details that differed from lender to lender, and lots of choices to make.

The only common thing was the warning that my house probably wouldn't qualify for a fixed interest rate, nor would I. The house is too small to carry paper into the federal mortgage market where most fixed-rate loans end up. And my income is too small to make the payments on anything but the funny-money mortgages that have artificially lowered payments at the beginning.

There were so many possibilities within those limits, I think maybe I'm actually glad the real estate person specified a particular mortgage company. It saved me lots of boring decisions.

God knows, it's going to be hard enough to move away from the bay view I now rent.

And packing will be agonizing.

And then there's a housewarming to plan.

Fortunately, my Sunday afternoons will be available.

184

It Can be Hard
To Say Goodbye

Sure, just when I'm trying to say goodbye to Lovers Point, some bizarre jade plant down there has to pop out in the prettiest bloom in the world.

It looks like tiny, yellow daisies, hundreds of them clumped together in a cluster about the size and shape of a pineapple. Delicate little things, all huddled together.

I found just one plant like that, tucked behind big bushes at the edge of a cliff.

I don't know what it is and I don't need to. I can worship beauty just fine in ignorance.

But this gorgeous bloom has suddenly appeared to make me wonder how many more delights might be getting ready to pop out just as I leave.

Am I moving at the wrong time? There are real misgivings about moving away from a place as beautiful as Lovers Point.

Oh, I know I'm not going that far and it doesn't have to be forever. But a few blocks — four, I think it is — can be a real barrier in a world where so many things compete for time.

I've been able to simply look out my apartment window and be drawn into infinite. There is that beautiful bay, with colors and movements that entice me to make time for a walk and a closer look, to see how the water splashes against the shore today, to monitor the otters and to look for jade blossoms along the cliffs.

But now that I'm moving a few blocks away, I'm afraid I won't see the water so much, won't be coaxed to make so much time for it. And I'm afraid I'll miss it.

My new house looks out on a tiny yard, a crowded street and a lot of other houses. I don't think I'll look out and see yard work calling to me, or a car that needs washing or anything like that. What I'm afraid of, though, is that I won't see anything compelling and I'll just stay in and write a letter or read a magazine or turn on the television, things I haven't found too much time for while there's been an ocean to watch.

I will miss that.

But after all the trouble I've had finding a charming house I can afford, no matter how small, I'm not going to let myself feel victimized because I have to move away from my bay view. At least, I hope not.

There are actually a few things I'm pleased to leave behind. Three noisy mufflers have moved onto my block in recent months. Two day-workers have moved in upstairs. And the landlord has been building a fence outside my bedroom window for the past several weekends.

Oh, none of that's particularly bad. But the noisy mufflers wake me up once in a while. And the neighbors sometimes compete for water pressure when I'm taking a shower. And there's no sense of privacy when people walk around outside your ground-floor windows, whether or not they are hammering and sawing.

That makes a bedroom at the back of a house in which I control access and water faucets seem especially delightful right now, even if it means giving up my ocean view. All life is a trade-off, I guess.

And the actual business of moving on the Peninsula has turned out to be fairly effortless, once I found a place and the paperwork was done.

The folks at San Francisco Federal Savings processed my mortgage application within two weeks.

That kind of efficiency got a commitment from the bank that left me free to set all sorts of dates and arrange details with certainty. It takes the guess-work, the panic and the last-minute frustrations out of buying a house and makes it almost civil.

The bank has been easy to deal with, and so have the sellers, the inspectors, the insurance company and all the stuff like that.

I haven't got around to the utilities yet, but I wouldn't expect problems with any of them except maybe the cable company. For the others, it's just a matter of calling and writing checks, I think.

But I've already had my problems with Monterey Peninsula TV Cable Television, so I wouldn't be surprised by more.

One time, the cable company disconnected my apartment by mistake when the neighbors moved. It took two days to get the crew back to redo it.

The other problems have all been billing errors — three in the eight months that I've lived here, a 37.5 percent error factor.

But if cable's the worst problem with this move, I'll float in the champagne.

As moving day gets closer, though, I'm starting to wonder about the mover I've hired for the job. He's really a firefighter who moves furniture as a side job. And I've just started to wonder whether he moves like everybody else — by carrying stuff through the door — or whether he just throws it through a broken window so his colleagues can hose it down in the yard.

Sure, it's probably just my imagination.

Fortunately, I don't have much time to worry about that. I've got to pack yet, and sort and throw out the stuff that's not going to fit into a one-bedroom house.

Of course, there's less junk to sort through on this move. I tidied my stuff to go from a six-room house with a garage to a four-room apartment with a closet. It's going to be fairly simple to get rid of enough to fit into a three-room house with a porch.

I really think it's easy to get rid of more furniture and dishes and knick-knacks. Material things have lost a lot of value since I've been living here.

I don't know if it's because I really don't like to hassle with it in the moving. Or if my values have changed in this natural paradise. Or if the prices for floor space have simply forced me to live with less.

But the rule now seems to be that if it doesn't have a vital function or a tremendous value, get rid of it.

Even the extra hangers in the closet.

Yes, the house is that small.

I've been taking stuff to antique dealers in Carmel and Pacific Grove, a consignment shop on Lighthouse Avenue, an auction house and used record stores in Monterey, the Salvation Army's Thrift Store in Seaside, relatives in Santa Cruz and friends in Sacramento.

But I'm getting down to the tough stuff. That's boxes of pictures and clippings that could crowd me out of the closet.

I've already found one box full of pictures and negatives that I shipped out from the East Coast 11 years ago and hadn't got around to opening yet. I even had warranties for cameras that I got rid of years ago. That box went almost intact to the dump.

There was another one that was tougher. It had pictures of people and places from long ago. And when I went through it, my mind froze on some of those faces and I could see whole scenes, feel some of the old moods again.

That box stirred some emotions I'm not sure I want stirred right now. And I wondered why pictures have to last longer than relationships.

I'm not suggesting we should forget the past. Necessarily. But I no longer have room for all of the mementoes.

188